Salads

This edition published in 2009

Love Food ® is an imprint of Parragon Books Ltd

Parragon
Queen Street House
4 Queen Street
Bath BA1 1HE, UK

Copyright © Parragon Books Ltd 2007
Love Food ® and the accompanying heart device is
a trademark of Parragon Books Ltd.

Photography by Günter Beer
Home Economist Stevan Paul
Design by Talking Design
Introduction and additional recipes written by
Beverly Le Blanc

ISBN 978-1-4075-6351-0

Printed in China

This book uses imperial, metric, and US cup
measurements. Follow the same units of
measurement throughout; do not mix imperial
and metric. All spoon measurements are
level, unless otherwise stated: teaspoons
are assumed to be 5ml, and tablespoons
are assumed to be 15ml. Unless otherwise
stated, milk is assumed to be whole, eggs and
individual fruits such as bananas are medium,
and pepper is freshly ground black pepper.

Recipes using raw or very lightly cooked eggs
should be avoided by infants, the elderly,
pregnant women, convalescents, and anyone
with a chronic condition. Pregnant and
breast-feeding women are advised to avoid
eating peanuts and peanut products.

contents

introduction   6

sunshine—a collection of vegetable salads   12

hearty—a collection of meat & poultry salads   64

sparkling—a collection of fish & seafood salads   116

health-boosting—a collection of energizing salads   168

index   222

The taste of summer all year round

Take a fresh look at salads and you'll see there are a lot of exciting developments in the salad bowl. Banished forever is the image of salads as dull diet food consisting of little more than limp lettuce and soggy, flavorless tomatoes.

Today, salads are one of the ultimate health foods. They can contain an exciting variety of colorful, delicious, and satisfying ingredients that provide the nutrients essential for healthy living. You'll find plenty of inspiration in this book for a cornucopia of healthy salads for all occasions, from light lunches and family meals to stylish dinner parties. And, remember, salads aren't just for summer. We have plenty of ideas for salads that brighten and lighten winter mealtimes, too. In fact, once you get into the habit of thinking "salad" while menu planning, ideas will also come to you whatever the time of the year as you push your shopping cart along the supermarket aisles or stop at the cheese counter or produce department.

Salads are versatile enough to cater for vegetarians and meat-eaters alike. Meat, seafood, and poultry are ideal salad ingredients, along with the perhaps more commonly used lettuce and other leaves, vegetables, fruit, herbs, nuts, seeds, grains, legumes, and cheese. And with so many ingredients to choose from, salads can be as simple and light or complex and filling as you like. They also have the added bonus that they are versatile enough to fit easily into all your meal plans, from first courses through to desserts.

As you flip through these recipes you'll find classic favorites—Caesar salad, chef's salad, and salad niçoise, to name a few—as well as fresh, new ideas that capture the flavors of cuisines around the world. If, for example, the idea of chicken salad doesn't excite because you've been making the same recipe out of habit for as long as you can remember, try Thai-Style Chicken Salad (page 102). You'll never think of chicken salad as humdrum again!

Bowls of Goodness

It wasn't long ago that when "salads" and "health" were linked it was in the context of weight-reducing diets that were restrictive and ultimately unsatisfying. Today, however, salads are a delicious component of a healthy diet, giving you endless variety at mealtimes without long hours in the kitchen.

With fresh produce from all corners of the globe readily available in supermarkets and gourmet food stores, you can enjoy a variety of salads all year round but, remember, salads are at their most flavorsome and nutritious when made with seasonal produce in its prime.

We are all being urged to eat more fruit and vegetables every day, and a salad a day can

go a long way to help you meet the minimum target of 2½ cups for adults. Enjoy a bowl of Traditional Greek Salad (page 17) or Three-Color Salad (page 34), for example, and you'll be more than halfway to success. What could be easier—or more enjoyable?

Salads also make great accompaniments, served alongside a filling bowl of pasta or a plate of hot or cold roast meat.

So, if you regularly fall back on the old favorite of just tossing a few green leaves with a simple oil-and-vinegar dressing, it's definitely time to think again. It's very easy to mix and match ingredients and the choice has never been greater. And don't make the mistake of thinking all salad ingredients have to be raw, either. Adding small amounts of cooked meat, poultry and seafood to lettuce leaves and other vegetables gives you a satisfying meal. If you want a meal-in-a-bowl, try Roast Pork with Pumpkin (page 113), Smoked Chicken Salad with Avocado & Tarragon Dressing (page 110), and Shrimp & Rice Salad (page 145), for example. There are plenty of vegetarian main-course salads, too, such as the Middle Eastern favorite Tabbouleh (page 190) and Buckwheat Noodle Salad with Smoked Tofu (page 193).

Cooked vegetables also make good salad ingredients. Grilled peppers, fried eggplants, blanched beans of all varieties, and peas are just some of the cooked vegetables you'll find adding flavor and an extra dimension to the salads in this book.

Colorful Greens

Even with so many ingredients to choose from, salad greens still provide the backbone of many popular salads. Take a look around your supermarket and you'll see leaves in many colors and textures, ranging from pearly, pale white Belgian endive to bright red and white radicchio. They also have a variety of flavors, from robust and peppery to sweet, nutty, and mild.

The greater the variety of leaves you include in your salad, the more interesting it will be, and the more nutrients it will contain. When you select salad leaves, remember that the darker colored ones, such as spinach leaves, contain more beta-carotene, which help fight some forms of cancer and other illnesses. Leafy green vegetables are also excellent sources of fiber.

It's become very convenient to grab a bag of mixed salad leaves at the supermarket, but it can be more satisfying to sample a selection of greens sold separately at farmers' markets. Asian and other ethnic food stores are also a good source of unusual greens.

Try these new and familiar greens to add variety to your salad bowl:

• Arugula—known for its pronounced peppery flavor, these dark green leaves perk up many salads. Popular in Italian salads. Substitute watercress if you can't find arugula.

• Beet greens—distinctive with their ruby-red stems, these soft leaves are mildly flavored.

• Mâche—also labelled as corn salad or lamb's lettuce, these tender leaves have a mild, slightly nutty flavor.

• Mesclun or mesclum—now sold in supermarkets, this French mix of leaves can include arugula, chervil, dandelion, and oak-leaf lettuce. Just add dressing and toss.

• Mizuna—from the Far East, this winter green has a full peppery flavor. Its pointy green leaves add visual interest to salads, too.

• Nasturtium—use both the colorful flowers and peppery leaves in salads.

• Radicchio—there is nothing like the bright red and white leaves of this member of the bitter endive family to liven autumn and early winter salads. It has a crisp texture and nutty, peppery flavor.

• Red chard—like beet greens, these fiber-rich leaves have bright red stems and sometimes the leaves are tinged red as well.

• Romaine lettuce—Caesar salad (page 14) simply wouldn't be Caesar salad without these long, crisp leaves. Comes in a large, compact head with long, crisp leaves that have a sweet nutty flavor.

Keep It Fresh

Good salads are only made with good ingredients, and freshness is all-important when buying salad greens. Because of the leaves' high water content, they are very perishable, so buy them as close as possible to serving. Not only will they taste best, they contain the most nutrients when they are in peak condition.

Let your eyes guide you when shopping for salad greens—fresh leaves look fresh. They won't have any leaves tinged with brown, nor will they be wilted or slimy.

When you get salad ingredients home, give them a rinse in cold water, then spin them dry or use a tea cloth to pat them dry. Never leave them to soak in a sink of cold water because all the water-soluble vitamins and minerals will leech out.

Use leafy ingredients as soon as possible, but most will keep for up to four days in a sealed container in the refrigerator. Once you open bags of prepared leaves, however, they should be used within 24 hours. You can prepare salad greens several hours in advance and store in the refrigerator, but do not dress until just before serving, because the acid in most dressings causes the leaves to wilt and become unappetizing.

sunshine

a collection of vegetable salads

caesar salad

serves 4

ingredients

²⁄₃ cup olive oil

2 garlic cloves

5 slices white bread, crusts removed,
 cut into ¹⁄₂-inch/1-cm cubes

1 large egg

2 romaine lettuces or 3 Boston lettuces

2 tbsp lemon juice

salt and pepper

8 canned anchovy fillets, drained and
 coarsely chopped

³⁄₄ cup fresh Parmesan cheese shavings

Bring a small, heavy-bottom pan of water to a boil.

Meanwhile, heat 4 tablespoons of the olive oil in a heavy-bottom skillet. Add the garlic and cubed bread and cook, stirring and tossing frequently, for 4–5 minutes, or until the bread is crispy and golden all over. Remove from the skillet with a slotted spoon and drain on paper towels.

Add the egg to the boiling water and cook for 1 minute, then remove from the pan and set aside.

Arrange the salad greens in a salad bowl. Mix the remaining olive oil and lemon juice together, then season to taste with salt and pepper. Crack the egg into the dressing and whisk to blend. Pour the dressing over the salad greens, toss well, then add the croutons and chopped anchovies and toss the salad again. Sprinkle with Parmesan cheese shavings and serve.

traditional greek salad

serves 4

ingredients

7 oz/200 g Greek feta cheese

½ head of iceberg lettuce or 1 lettuce
such as romaine or escarole, shredded
or sliced

4 tomatoes, cut into fourths

½ cucumber, sliced

12 Greek black olives, pitted

2 tbsp chopped fresh herbs, such as
oregano, flat-leaf parsley, mint, or basil

for the dressing

6 tbsp extra-virgin olive oil

2 tbsp fresh lemon juice

1 garlic clove, crushed

pinch of sugar

salt and pepper

Make the dressing by whisking together the oil, lemon juice, garlic, sugar, salt, and pepper, in a small bowl. Set aside. Cut the feta cheese into cubes about 1 inch/2.5 cm square. Put the lettuce, tomatoes, and cucumber in a salad bowl. Scatter over the cheese and toss together.

Just before serving, whisk the dressing, pour over the salad greens, and toss together. Scatter over the olives and chopped herbs and serve.

mozzarella salad with sun-dried tomatoes

serves 4

ingredients

3½ oz/100 g mixed salad greens, such
    as oak leaf lettuce, baby spinach, and
    arugula

1 lb 2 oz/500 g smoked mozzarella
    cheese, sliced

for the dressing

5 oz/140 g sun-dried tomatoes in olive oil
    (drained weight), reserving the oil from
    the jar

¼ cup coarsely shredded fresh basil

¼ cup coarsely chopped fresh flat-leaf
    parsley

1 tbsp capers, rinsed

1 tbsp balsamic vinegar

1 garlic clove, coarsely chopped

extra olive oil, if necessary

pepper

Put the sun-dried tomatoes, basil, parsley, capers, vinegar, and garlic in a food processor or blender. Measure the oil from the sun-dried tomatoes jar and make it up to ⅔ cup with more olive oil if necessary. Add it to the food processor or blender and process until smooth. Season to taste with pepper.

Divide the salad greens among 4 individual serving plates. Top with the slices of mozzarella and spoon the dressing over them. Serve immediately.

red & green salad

serves 4

ingredients

1 lb 7 oz/650 g cooked beet

3 tbsp extra-virgin olive oil

juice of 1 orange

1 tsp superfine sugar

1 tsp fennel seeds

salt and pepper

4 oz/115 g fresh baby spinach leaves

Using a sharp knife, dice the cooked beet and set aside until required. Heat the olive oil in a small, heavy-bottom pan. Add the orange juice, sugar and fennel seeds and season to taste with salt and pepper. Stir constantly until the sugar has dissolved.

Add the reserved beet to the pan and stir gently to coat. Remove the pan from the heat.

Arrange the baby spinach leaves in a large salad bowl. Spoon the warmed beet on top and serve immediately.

roasted garlic, sweet potato, broiled eggplant & bell pepper salad with mozzarella

serves 4

ingredients

2 sweet potatoes, peeled and cut into
    chunks

2 tbsp olive oil

pepper

2 garlic cloves, crushed

1 large eggplant, sliced

2 red bell peppers, seeded and sliced

7 oz/200 g mixed salad greens

2 x 5$\frac{1}{2}$ oz/150 g mozzarella cheeses,
    drained and sliced

for the dressing

1 tbsp balsamic vinegar

1 garlic clove, crushed

3 tbsp olive oil

1 small shallot, finely chopped

2 tbsp chopped mixed fresh herbs,
    such as tarragon, chervil, and basil

pepper

Preheat the oven to 375°F/190°C. Put the sweet potato chunks into a roasting pan with the oil, pepper to taste, and garlic and toss to combine. Roast in the preheated oven for 30 minutes, or until soft and slightly charred.

Meanwhile, preheat the broiler to high. Arrange the eggplant and bell pepper slices on the broiler pan and cook under the preheated broiler, turning occasionally, for 10 minutes, or until soft and slightly charred.

To make the dressing, whisk the vinegar, garlic, and oil together in a small bowl and stir in the shallot and herbs. Season to taste with pepper.

To serve, divide the salad greens among 4 serving plates and arrange the sweet potato, eggplant, bell peppers, and mozzarella on top. Drizzle with the dressing and serve.

mixed mushroom salad

serves 4

ingredients

3 tbsp pine nuts

2 red onions, cut into chunks

4 tbsp olive oil

2 garlic cloves, crushed

3 slices whole wheat bread, cubed

7 oz/200 g mixed salad greens

9 oz/250 g cremini mushrooms, sliced

5½ oz/150 g shiitake mushrooms, sliced

5½ oz/150 g oyster mushrooms, torn

for the dressing

1 garlic clove, crushed

2 tbsp red wine vinegar

4 tbsp walnut oil

1 tbsp finely chopped fresh parsley

pepper

Preheat the oven to 350°F/180°C. Heat a nonstick skillet over medium heat, add the pine nuts, and cook, turning, until just browned. Tip into a bowl and set aside.

Put the onions and 1 tablespoon of the olive oil into a roasting pan and toss to coat. Roast in the preheated oven for 30 minutes.

Meanwhile, heat 1 tablespoon of the remaining oil with the garlic in the nonstick skillet over high heat. Add the bread and cook, turning frequently, for 5 minutes, or until brown and crisp. Remove from the skillet and set aside.

Divide the salad greens among 4 serving plates and add the roasted onions. To make the dressing, whisk the garlic, vinegar, and oil together in a small bowl. Stir in the parsley and season to taste with pepper. Drizzle over the salad and onions.

Heat the remaining oil in a skillet, add the cremini and shiitake mushrooms, and cook for 2–3 minutes, stirring frequently. Add the oyster mushrooms and cook for an additional 2–3 minutes. Divide the hot mushroom mixture among the 4 plates. Sprinkle over the pine nuts and croutons and serve.

warm red lentil salad with goat cheese

serves 4

ingredients

2 tbsp olive oil

2 tsp cumin seeds

2 garlic cloves, crushed

2 tsp grated fresh gingerroot

1½ cups split red lentils

3 cups vegetable stock

2 tbsp chopped fresh mint

2 tbsp chopped fresh cilantro

2 red onions, thinly sliced

4⅜ cups baby spinach leaves

1 tsp hazelnut oil

5½ oz/150 g soft goat cheese

4 tbsp strained plain yogurt

pepper

Heat half the olive oil in a large skillet over medium heat, add the cumin seeds, garlic, and gingerroot and cook for 2 minutes, stirring constantly.

Stir in the lentils, then add the stock, a ladleful at a time, until it is all absorbed, stirring constantly—this will take about 20 minutes. Remove from the heat and stir in the herbs.

Meanwhile, heat the remaining olive oil in a skillet over medium heat, add the onions, and cook, stirring frequently, for 10 minutes, or until soft and lightly browned.

Toss the spinach in the hazelnut oil in a bowl, then divide among 4 serving plates.

Mash the goat cheese with the yogurt in a small bowl and season to taste with pepper.

Divide the lentils among the serving plates and top with the onions and goat cheese mixture.

green bean & walnut salad

serves 2

ingredients

1 lb/450 g green beans

1 small onion, finely chopped

1 garlic clove, chopped

4 tbsp freshly grated Parmesan cheese

2 tbsp chopped walnuts or almonds,
  to garnish

for the dressing

6 tbsp olive oil

2 tbsp white wine vinegar

salt and pepper

2 tsp chopped fresh tarragon

Trim the beans, but leave them whole. Cook for 3–4 minutes in salted boiling water. Drain well, refresh under cold running water, and drain again. Put into a mixing bowl and add the onion, garlic, and cheese.

Place the dressing ingredients in a jar with a screw-top lid. Shake well. Pour the dressing over the salad and toss gently to coat. Cover with plastic wrap and chill for at least 30 minutes. Remove the beans from the refrigerator 10 minutes before serving. Give them a quick stir and transfer to attractive serving dishes.

Toast the nuts in a dry skillet over medium heat for 2 minutes, or until they begin to brown. Sprinkle the toasted nuts over the beans to garnish before serving.

red onion, tomato & herb salad

serves 4

ingredients

2 lb/900 g tomatoes, sliced thinly

1 tbsp sugar (optional)

salt and pepper

1 red onion, sliced thinly

large handful coarsely chopped fresh herbs

for the dressing

2–4 tbsp vegetable oil

2 tbsp red wine vinegar or fruit vinegar

Arrange the tomato slices in a shallow bowl. Sprinkle with sugar (if using), salt, and pepper.

Separate the onion slices into rings and sprinkle them over the tomatoes. Sprinkle the herbs over the top. Any fresh herbs that are in season can be used—for example, tarragon, sorrel, cilantro, or basil.

Place the dressing ingredients in a jar with a screw-top lid. Shake well. Pour the dressing over the salad and mix gently. Cover with plastic wrap and chill for 20 minutes. Remove the salad from the refrigerator 5 minutes before serving.

nutty beet salad

serves 4

ingredients

3 tbsp red wine vinegar or fruit vinegar

3 cooked beets, grated

2 sharp eating apples

2 tbsp lemon juice

4 large handfuls mixed salad greens,
  to serve

4 tbsp pecans, to garnish

for the dressing

1/4 cup plain yogurt

1/4 cup mayonnaise

1 garlic clove, chopped

1 tbsp chopped fresh dill

salt and pepper

Sprinkle vinegar over the beets, cover with plastic wrap, and chill for at least 4 hours.

Core and slice the apples, place the slices in a dish, and sprinkle with the lemon juice to prevent discoloration.

Combine the dressing ingredients in a small bowl. Remove the beets from the refrigerator and dress. Add the apples to the beets and mix gently to coat with the salad dressing.

To serve, arrange a handful of salad greens on each plate and top with a large spoonful of the apple and beet mixture.

Toast the pecans in a heavy, dry skillet over medium heat for 2 minutes, or until they begin to brown. Sprinkle them over the beets and apple to garnish.

three-color salad

serves 4

ingredients

10 oz/280 g buffalo mozzarella, drained
   and thinly sliced

8 large tomatoes, sliced

salt and pepper

20 fresh basil leaves

1/2 cup extra-virgin olive oil

Arrange the mozzarella and tomato slices on 4 individual serving plates and season to taste with salt. Set aside in a cool place for 30 minutes.

Sprinkle the basil leaves over the salad and drizzle with the olive oil. Season with pepper and serve immediately.

broiled bell pepper salad

serves 4–6

ingredients

6 large red, orange, or yellow bell peppers,
    each cut in half lengthwise, broiled,
    and skinned
4 hard-cooked eggs, shelled
12 anchovy fillets in oil, drained
12 large black olives, pitted
extra-virgin olive oil or garlic-flavored
    olive oil, for drizzling
sherry vinegar, to taste
salt and pepper
crusty bread, to serve

Remove any cores and seeds from the broiled bell peppers and cut the flesh into thin strips. Arrange on a serving platter.

Cut the eggs into wedges and arrange over the bell pepper strips, along with the anchovy fillets and olives.

Drizzle oil over the top, then splash with sherry vinegar, adding both to taste. Sprinkle a little salt and pepper over the top and serve with crusty bread.

tomato salad with feta cheese

serves 4

ingredients

12 plum tomatoes, sliced

1 very small red onion, thinly sliced

½ oz/15 g arugula leaves

20 Greek black olives, pitted

7 oz/200 g Greek feta cheese

1 egg

3 tbsp all-purpose flour

2 tbsp olive oil

for the dressing

3 tbsp extra-virgin olive oil

juice of ½ lemon

2 tsp chopped fresh oregano

pinch of sugar

pepper

Make the dressing by whisking together the extra-virgin olive oil, the lemon juice, oregano, sugar, and black pepper in a pitcher or small bowl. Set aside.

Prepare the salad by arranging the tomatoes, onion, arugula, and olives on 4 individual plates.

Cut the feta cheese into cubes about 1 inch/2.5 cm square. Beat the egg in a dish and put the flour on a separate plate. Coat the cheese in the egg, shake off the excess, and then coat in the flour.

Heat the olive oil in a large skillet, add the cheese, and cook over medium heat, turning over the cubes of cheese until they are golden on all sides.

Scatter the fried feta over the salad. Whisk together the prepared dressing, spoon over the salad, and serve warm.

broiled bell pepper &
goat cheese salad

serves 4

ingredients

2 red bell peppers

2 green bell peppers

2 yellow or orange bell peppers

½ cup vinaigrette or herb vinaigrette

6 scallions, finely chopped

1 tbsp capers in brine, rinsed

7 oz/200 g soft goat cheese,
   any rind removed

fresh flat-leaf parsley, chopped, to serve

Preheat the broiler to high. Arrange the bell peppers on a broiler pan, position about 4 inches/10 cm from the heat, and broil for 8–10 minutes, turning them frequently, until the skins are charred all over. Transfer the bell peppers to a bowl, cover with a damp dish towel, and let stand until cool enough to handle.

Using a small knife, skin each of the bell peppers. Working over a bowl to catch the juices from inside the bell peppers, cut each one in half and remove the cores and seeds, then cut the flesh into thin strips.

Arrange the bell peppers on a serving platter and spoon over the reserved juices, then add the vinaigrette. Sprinkle over the scallions and capers, then crumble over the cheese. If not serving immediately, cover with plastic wrap and chill until required. Sprinkle with the parsley to serve.

fava bean salad

ingredients

3 lb/1.3 kg fresh young fava beans, or
  1½ lb/675 g frozen baby fava beans

1½ cups crumbled Greek feta cheese

1 bunch of scallions, thinly sliced

2 tbsp chopped fresh dill or mint

2 hard-cooked eggs, cut into fourths

crusty bread

strained plain yogurt, to serve (optional)

for the dressing

6 tbsp extra-virgin olive oil

grated zest of 1 lemon and
  2 tbsp lemon juice

1 small garlic clove, crushed

pinch of sugar

pepper

Make the dressing by whisking together the oil, lemon zest and juice, garlic, sugar, and black pepper in a small bowl. Set aside. Shell the fresh fava beans, if using, and cook in boiling salted water for 5–10 minutes, or until tender. If using frozen fava beans, cook in boiling salted water for 4–5 minutes. Drain the cooked beans and put in a salad bowl.

Whisk the dressing and pour over the beans while they are still warm. Spinkle over the feta cheese, add the scallions, and toss together. Sprinkle over the chopped dill and arrange the egg fourths in the bowl.

Serve warm with crusty bread and a bowl of yogurt to spoon on top, if wished.

mexican tomato salad

serves 4

ingredients

1 lb 5 oz/600 g tomatoes, peeled, seeded,
    and coarsely chopped

1 onion, thinly sliced and pushed
    out into rings

14 oz/400 g canned kidney beans,
    drained and rinsed

for the dressing

1 fresh green chile, seeded and diced

3 tbsp chopped fresh cilantro

3 tbsp olive oil

1 garlic clove, finely chopped

4 tbsp lime juice

salt and pepper

Place the chopped tomatoes and onion slices in a large serving
bowl and mix well. Stir in the kidney beans.

Mix the chile, cilantro, olive oil, garlic, and lime juice together in
a measuring cup and season to taste with salt and pepper.

Pour the dressing over the salad and toss thoroughly. Serve
immediately or cover with plastic wrap and let chill in the
refrigerator until required.

thai noodle salad

serves 4

ingredients

1 oz/25 g dried wood ears

2 oz/55 g dried Chinese mushrooms

4 oz/115 g cellophane noodles

½ cup cooked lean ground pork

4 oz/115 g shelled raw shrimp

5 fresh red chiles, seeded and thinly sliced

1 tbsp chopped fresh cilantro

3 tbsp Thai fish sauce

3 tbsp lime juice

1 tbsp brown sugar

Put the wood ears and Chinese mushrooms in separate bowls and pour over enough boiling water to cover. Let soak for 30 minutes. After 20 minutes, put the cellophane noodles in a separate bowl and pour over enough hot water to cover. Let the noodles soak for 10 minutes, or according to the package instructions.

Drain the wood ears, rinse thoroughly and cut into small pieces. Drain the mushrooms, squeezing out as much liquid as possible. Cut off and discard the stalks and cut the caps in half. Pour just enough water into a pan to cover the bottom and bring to a boil. Add the pork, shrimp, wood ears, and mushrooms and let simmer, stirring, for 3 minutes, or until cooked through. Drain well. Drain the noodles and cut them into short lengths with scissors.

Put the chiles, cilantro, fish sauce, lime juice, and brown sugar in a salad bowl and stir until the sugar has dissolved. Add the noodles and the shrimp and pork mixture, toss well, and serve.

sweet potato & bean salad

serves 4

ingredients

1 sweet potato

4 baby carrots, halved

4 tomatoes

4 celery stalks, chopped

8 oz/225 g canned cranberry beans,
   drained and rinsed

4 oz/115 g mixed salad greens,
   such as frisée, arugula, radicchio
   and oak leaf lettuce

1 tbsp golden raisins

4 scallions, sliced diagonally

for the dressing

2 tbsp lemon juice

1 garlic clove, crushed

5 fl oz/150 ml plain yogurt

2 tbsp olive oil

salt and pepper

Peel and dice the sweet potato. Bring a pan of water to a boil over medium heat. Add the sweet potato and cook for 10 minutes, until tender. Drain the potato, transfer to a bowl, and set aside.

Cook the carrots in a separate pan of boiling water for 1 minute. Drain thoroughly and add to the sweet potato. Cut the tops off the tomatoes and scoop out the seeds. Chop the flesh and add to the bowl with the celery and beans. Mix well.

Line a large serving bowl with the mixed salad greens. Spoon the sweet potato and bean mixture on top, then sprinkle with the golden raisins and scallions.

Put all the dressing ingredients in a screw-top jar, with salt and pepper to taste, screw on the lid and shake until well blended. Pour over the salad and serve.

raspberry & feta salad with couscous

serves 6

ingredients

12 oz/350 g couscous

2½ cups boiling chicken stock or
   vegetable stock

12 oz/350 g fresh raspberries

small bunch of fresh basil

8 oz/225 g feta cheese, cubed or crumbled

2 zucchini, thinly sliced

4 scallions, trimmed and diagonally sliced

⅓ cup pine nuts, toasted

grated rind of 1 lemon

for the dressing

1 tbsp white wine vinegar

1 tbsp balsamic vinegar

4 tbsp extra-virgin
olive oil

juice of 1 lemon

salt and pepper

Put the couscous in a large heatproof bowl and pour over the stock. Stir well, then cover and let soak until all the stock has been absorbed.

Pick over the raspberries, discarding any that are overripe. Shred the basil leaves.

Transfer the couscous to a large serving bowl and stir well to break up any lumps. Add the cheese, zucchini, scallions, raspberries, and pine nuts. Stir in the basil and lemon rind and gently toss all the ingredients together.

Put all the dressing ingredients in a screw-top jar, with salt and pepper to taste, then screw on the lid and shake until well blended. Pour over the salad and serve.

orecchiette salad with pears & bleu cheese

serves 4

ingredients

9 oz/250 g dried orecchiette

1 head radicchio, torn into pieces

1 oak leaf lettuce, torn into pieces

2 pears

1 tbsp lemon juice

9 oz/250 g bleu cheese, diced

scant $\frac{1}{2}$ cup chopped walnuts

4 tomatoes, quartered

1 red onion, sliced

1 carrot, grated

8 fresh basil leaves

2 oz/55 g corn salad

for the dressing

4 tbsp olive oil

2 tbsp lemon juice

salt and pepper

Bring a large heavy-bottom pan of lightly salted water to a boil. Add the pasta, return to a boil, and cook for 8–10 minutes, or until tender but still firm to the bite. Drain, refresh in a bowl of cold water and drain again.

Place the radicchio and oak leaf lettuce leaves in a large bowl. Halve the pears, remove the cores, and dice the flesh. Toss the diced pear with 1 tablespoon of lemon juice in a small bowl to prevent discoloration. Top the salad with the bleu cheese, walnuts, pears, pasta, tomatoes, onion slices, and grated carrot. Add the basil and corn salad.

For the dressing, mix the lemon juice and the olive oil together in a measuring cup, then season to taste with salt and pepper. Pour the dressing over the salad, toss, and serve.

salad with garlic dressing

serves 4

ingredients

3 oz/85 g cucumber, cut into batons

6 scallions, halved

2 tomatoes, seeded and
    cut into 8 wedges

1 yellow bell pepper, seeded and
    cut into strips

2 celery stalks, cut into strips

4 radishes, quartered

3 oz/85 g arugula

1 tbsp chopped fresh mint,
    to garnish (optional)

for the dressing

2 tbsp lemon juice

1 garlic clove, crushed

$\frac{2}{3}$ cup plain yogurt

2 tbsp olive oil

salt and pepper

To make the salad, gently mix the cucumber batons, scallions, tomato wedges, yellow bell pepper strips, celery strips, radishes, and arugula in a large serving bowl.

To make the dressing, stir the lemon juice, garlic, plain yogurt, and olive oil together in a small bowl until thoroughly combined. Season with salt and pepper to taste.

Spoon the dressing over the salad and toss to mix. Sprinkle the salad with chopped mint (if using) and serve.

warm pasta salad

serves 4

ingredients

8 oz/225 g dried farfalle or
    other pasta shapes
6 pieces of sun-dried tomato in oil,
    drained and chopped
4 scallions, chopped
1¼ cups arugula, shredded
½ cucumber, seeded and diced
salt and pepper

for the dressing

4 tbsp olive oil
1 tbsp white wine vinegar
½ tsp superfine sugar
1 tsp Dijon mustard
salt and pepper
4 fresh basil leaves, finely shredded

To make the dressing, whisk the olive oil, vinegar, sugar, and mustard together in a bowl or pitcher. Season to taste with salt and pepper and stir in the basil.

Bring a large heavy-bottom pan of lightly salted water to a boil. Add the pasta, return to a boil, and cook for 8–10 minutes, or until tender but still firm to the bite. Drain and transfer to a salad bowl. Add the dressing and toss well.

Add the tomatoes, scallions, arugula, and cucumber, season to taste with salt and pepper, and toss. Serve warm.

italian salad

serves 4

ingredients

8 oz/225 g dried conchiglie

1¾ oz/50 g pine nuts

12 oz/350 g cherry tomatoes, cut in half

1 red bell pepper, seeded and
    cut into bite-size chunks

1 red onion, chopped

7 oz/200 g buffalo mozzarella, cubed

12 black olives, pitted

1 oz/25 g fresh basil leaves

shavings of fresh Parmesan cheese,
    to garnish

crusty bread, to serve

for the dressing

5 tbsp extra-virgin olive oil

2 tbsp balsamic vinegar

1 tbsp chopped fresh basil

salt and pepper

Bring a large pan of lightly salted water to a boil. Add the pasta and cook over medium heat for about 10 minutes, or according to the package instructions. When cooked, the pasta should be tender but still firm to the bite. Drain, rinse under cold running water, and drain again. Let cool.

While the pasta is cooking, put the pine nuts in a dry skillet and cook over low heat for 1–2 minutes, until golden brown. Remove from the heat, transfer to a dish, and let cool.

To make the dressing, put the oil, vinegar, and basil into a small bowl. Season with salt and pepper and stir together well. Cover with plastic wrap and set to one side.

To assemble the salad, divide the pasta among serving bowls. Add the pine nuts, tomatoes, red bell pepper, onion, cheese, and olives. Scatter over the basil leaves, then drizzle over the dressing. Garnish with fresh Parmesan cheese shavings and serve with crusty bread.

potato salad

serves 4

ingredients

1 lb 9 oz/700 g new potatoes

8 scallions

1 cup mayonnaise

1 tsp paprika

salt and pepper

2 tbsp snipped fresh chives

pinch of paprika, to garnish

Bring a large pan of lightly salted water to a boil. Add the potatoes and cook for 10–15 minutes, or until just tender.

Drain the potatoes and rinse them under cold running water until completely cold. Drain again. Transfer the potatoes to a bowl and reserve until required.

Using a sharp knife, slice the scallions thinly on the diagonal.

Mix the mayonnaise, paprika, and salt and pepper to taste together in a bowl. Pour the mixture over the potatoes. Add the scallions to the potatoes and toss together.

Transfer the potato salad to a serving bowl and sprinkle with snipped chives and a pinch of paprika. Cover and let chill in the refrigerator until required.

capri salad

serves 4

ingredients

2 beefsteak tomatoes

4½ oz/125 g mozzarella cheese

12 black olives

8 fresh basil leaves

1 tbsp balsamic vinegar

1 tbsp extra-virgin olive oil

salt and pepper

fresh basil leaves, to garnish

Using a sharp knife, cut the tomatoes into thin slices. Drain the mozzarella, if necessary, and cut into slices and stone the black olives before slicing into rings.

Layer the tomatoes, mozzarella slices, olives, and basil leaves in 4 stacks, finishing with a layer of cheese on top.

Place each stack under a preheated hot broiler for 2–3 minutes or just long enough to melt the mozzarella.

Drizzle over the balsamic vinegar and olive oil, and season to taste with a little salt and pepper.

Transfer to individual serving plates and garnish with fresh basil leaves. Serve immediately.

hearty

a collection of meat & poultry salads

waldorf summer chicken salad

serves 4

ingredients

1 lb 2 oz red dessert apples, diced

3 tbsp fresh lemon juice

⅔ cup light mayonnaise

1 head celery

4 shallots, sliced

1 garlic clove, finely chopped

¾ cup walnuts, chopped

1 lb 2 oz cooked chicken, cubed

1 cos lettuce

pepper

chopped walnuts, to garnish

Place the apples in a bowl with the lemon juice and 1 tablespoon of mayonnaise. Leave for 40 minutes.

Using a sharp knife, slice the celery very thinly. Add the celery, shallots, garlic, and walnuts to the apple and mix together. Stir in the mayonnaise and blend thoroughly.

Add the cooked chicken to the bowl and mix well.

Line a serving dish with the lettuce. Pile the chicken salad into a serving bowl, sprinkle with pepper and garnish with the chopped walnuts.

chef's salad

serves 6

ingredients

1 iceberg lettuce, shredded

6 oz/175 g cooked lean ham,
  cut into thin strips

6 oz/175 g cooked tongue,
  cut into thin strips

12 oz/350 g cooked chicken,
  cut into thin strips

6 oz/175 g Gruyère cheese

4 tomatoes, quartered

3 hard-cooked eggs, shelled and quartered

1¾ cups Thousand Island dressing

sliced French bread, to serve

Arrange the lettuce on a large serving platter. Arrange the cold meats decoratively on top.

Cut the Gruyère cheese into thin cubes.

Arrange the thin cheese sticks over the salad, and the tomato and egg quarters around the edge of the platter. Serve the salad immediately with the Thousand Island dressing and sliced French bread.

prosciutto with melon & asparagus

ingredients

8 oz/225 g asparagus spears

1 small or ½ medium-size Galia or
    cantaloupe melon

2 oz/55 g prosciutto, thinly sliced

5½ oz/150 g bag mixed salad greens,
    such as herb salad with arugula

⅝ cup fresh raspberries

1 tbsp freshly shaved Parmesan cheese

for the dressing

1 tbsp balsamic vinegar

2 tbsp raspberry vinegar

2 tbsp orange juice

Trim the asparagus, cutting in half if very long. Cook in lightly salted boiling water over medium heat for 5 minutes, or until tender. Drain and plunge into cold water, then drain again and set aside.

Cut the melon in half and scoop out the seeds. Cut into small wedges and cut away the rind. Separate the prosciutto slices, cut in half and wrap around the melon wedges.

Arrange the salad greens on a large serving platter and place the melon wedges on top together with the asparagus spears.

Scatter over the raspberries and Parmesan shavings. Place the vinegars and juice in a screw-top jar and shake until blended. Pour over the salad and serve.

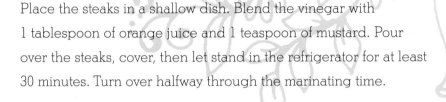

warm beef niçoise

serves 4

ingredients

4 tenderloin steaks, about 4 oz/115 g each,
    fat discarded

2 tbsp red wine vinegar

2 tbsp orange juice

2 tsp ready-made English mustard

2 eggs

6 oz/175 g new potatoes

4 oz/115 g green beans, trimmed

6 oz/175 g mixed salad greens, such as
    baby spinach, arugula, and mizuna

1 yellow bell pepper, seeded, peeled,
    and cut into strips

6 oz/175 g cherry tomatoes, halved

black olives, pitted, to garnish (optional)

2 tsp extra-virgin olive oil

Place the steaks in a shallow dish. Blend the vinegar with
1 tablespoon of orange juice and 1 teaspoon of mustard. Pour
over the steaks, cover, then let stand in the refrigerator for at least
30 minutes. Turn over halfway through the marinating time.

Place the eggs in a pan and cover with cold water. Bring to a
boil, then reduce the heat to a simmer and cook for 10 minutes.
Remove and plunge the eggs into cold water. Once cold, shell
and set aside.

Meanwhile, place the potatoes in a pan and cover with cold
water. Bring to a boil, then cover and let simmer for 15 minutes,
or until tender when pierced with a fork. Drain and set aside.

Bring a saucepan of water to the boil, add the beans and cook for
5 minutes, or until just tender. Drain, plunge into cold water and
drain again. Arrange the potatoes and beans on top of the salad
leaves together with the bell pepper, cherry tomatoes, and olives,
if using. Blend the remaining orange juice and mustard with the
olive oil and set aside.

Heat a stovetop grill pan or griddle until smoking. Drain the
steaks and cook for 3–5 minutes on each side or according to
personal preference. Slice the steaks and arrange on top of the
salad, then pour over the dressing and serve.

cajun chicken salad

serves 4

ingredients

4 skinless, boneless chicken breasts,
    about 5 oz/140 g each

4 tsp Cajun seasoning

2 tsp corn oil (optional)

1 ripe mango, peeled, seeded, and
    cut into thick slices

7 oz/200 g mixed salad greens

1 red onion, thinly sliced and cut in half

6 oz/175 g cooked beet, diced

3 oz/85 g radishes, sliced

generous ⅜ cup walnut halves

2 tbsp sesame seeds, to garnish

for the dressing

4 tbsp walnut oil

1–2 tsp Dijon mustard

1 tbsp lemon juice

salt and pepper

Make 3 diagonal slashes across each chicken breast. Put the chicken into a shallow dish and sprinkle all over with the Cajun seasoning. Cover and let chill for at least 30 minutes.

When ready to cook, brush a stove-top grill pan with the corn oil, if using. Heat over high heat until very hot and a few drops of water sprinkled into the pan sizzle immediately. Add the chicken and cook for 7–8 minutes on each side, or until thoroughly cooked. If still slightly pink in the center, cook a little longer. Remove the chicken and set aside.

Add the mango slices to the pan and cook for 2 minutes on each side. Remove and set aside.

Meanwhile, arrange the salad greens in a salad bowl and sprinkle over the onion, beet, radishes, and walnut halves.

Put the walnut oil, mustard, lemon juice, and salt and pepper to taste in a screw-top jar and shake until well blended. Pour over the salad.

Arrange the mango and the salad on the serving plate, top with the chicken breast and sprinkle with sesame seeds.

roast beef salad

serves 4

ingredients

1 lb 10 oz/750 g beef fillet, trimmed
    of any visible fat

pepper

2 tsp Worcestershire sauce

3 tbsp olive oil

14 oz/400 g green beans

3½ oz/100 g small pasta,
    such as orecchiette

2 red onions, finely sliced

1 large head radicchio

generous ¼ cup green olives, pitted

scant ⅓ cup shelled hazelnuts, whole

for the dressing

1 tsp Dijon mustard

2 tbsp white wine vinegar

5 tbsp olive oil

Preheat the oven to 425°F/220°C. Rub the beef with pepper to taste and Worcestershire sauce. Heat 2 tablespoons of the oil in a small roasting pan over high heat, add the beef, and sear on all sides. Transfer the dish to the preheated oven and roast for 30 minutes. Remove and let cool.

Bring a large pan of water to a boil, add the beans, and cook for 5 minutes, or until just tender. Remove with a slotted spoon and refresh the beans under cold running water. Drain and put into a large bowl.

Return the bean cooking water to a boil, add the pasta, and cook for 11 minutes, or until tender. Drain, return to the pan, and toss with the remaining oil.

Add the pasta to the beans with the onions, radicchio leaves, olives, and hazelnuts, mix gently and transfer to a serving bowl or dish. Arrange some thinly sliced beef on top.

Whisk the dressing ingredients together in a separate bowl, then pour over the salad and serve at once with extra sliced beef.

walnut, pear & crispy bacon salad

serves 4

ingredients

4 lean bacon slices

generous 5/8 cup walnut halves

2 Red Bartlett pears, cored and
   sliced lengthwise

1 tbsp lemon juice

6 oz/175 g watercress,
   tough stalks removed

for the dressing

3 tbsp extra-virgin olive oil

2 tbsp lemon juice

1/2 tsp honey

salt and pepper

Preheat the broiler to high. Arrange the bacon on a foil-lined broiler pan and cook under the preheated broiler until well browned and crisp. Let cool, then cut into 1/2-inch/1-cm pieces.

Meanwhile, heat a dry skillet over medium heat and lightly toast the walnuts, shaking the skillet frequently, for 3 minutes, or until lightly browned. Let cool.

Toss the pears in the lemon juice to prevent discoloration. Put the watercress, walnuts, pears, and bacon into a salad bowl.

To make the dressing, whisk the oil, lemon juice, and honey together in a small bowl or pitcher. Season to taste with salt and pepper, then pour over the salad. Toss well to combine and serve.

warm chicken liver salad

serves 4

ingredients

salad greens

1 tbsp olive oil

1 small onion, chopped finely

1 lb/450 g frozen chicken livers, thawed

1 tsp chopped fresh tarragon

1 tsp whole-grain mustard

2 tbsp balsamic vinegar

salt and pepper

Arrange the salad greens on serving plates.

Heat the oil in a nonstick skillet, add the onion, and cook for
5 minutes, or until softened. Add the chicken livers, tarragon, and
mustard and cook for 3–5 minutes, stirring, until tender. Put on
top of the salad greens.

Add the vinegar, salt, and pepper to the skillet and heat, stirring
constantly, until all the sediment has been lifted from the skillet.
Pour the dressing over the chicken livers and serve warm.

artichoke & prosciutto salad

serves 4

ingredients

9¾ oz/275 g canned artichoke
    hearts in oil, drained
4 small tomatoes
1 oz/25 g sun-dried tomatoes
    in oil, drained
1½ oz/40 g prosciutto
1 tbsp pitted black olives, halved
handful of fresh basil sprigs
crusty bread, to serve

for the dressing

3 tbsp olive oil
1 tbsp white wine vinegar
1 garlic clove, crushed
½ tsp mild mustard
1 tsp honey
salt and pepper, to taste

Make sure the artichoke hearts are thoroughly drained, then cut them into quarters and place in a serving bowl. Cut each fresh tomato into wedges. Slice the sun-dried tomatoes into thin strips. Cut the prosciutto into thin strips and add to the bowl with the tomatoes and olive halves.

Keeping a few basil sprigs whole for garnishing, tear the remainder of the leaves into small pieces and add to the bowl containing the other salad ingredients.

To make the dressing, place all the ingredients in a screw-top jar and shake vigorously until they are well blended.

Pour the dressing over the salad and toss together. Garnish the salad with with a few basil sprigs and serve with crusty bread.

lima bean, onion & herb salad with spicy sausage

serves 2

ingredients

1 tbsp corn oil

1 small onion, finely sliced

9 oz/250 g canned lima beans, drained and rinsed

1 tsp balsamic vinegar

2 chorizo sausages, sliced diagonally

1 small tomato, diced

2 tbsp harissa paste

3 oz/85 g mixed herb salad

Heat the oil in a nonstick skillet over medium heat, add the onion, and cook, stirring frequently, until softened but not browned. Add the beans and cook for an additional 1 minute, then add the vinegar, stirring well. Keep warm.

Meanwhile, heat a separate dry skillet over medium heat, add the chorizo slices, and cook, turning occasionally, until lightly browned. Remove with a slotted spoon and drain on paper towels.

Mix the tomato and harissa paste together in a small bowl. Divide the herb salad between 2 plates, spoon over the bean mixture, and sprinkle over the warm chorizo slices. Top with a spoonful of the tomato and harissa mixture and serve at once.

turkey & rice salad

serves 4

ingredients

4 cups chicken stock

scant 1 cup mixed long-grain and wild rice

2 tbsp corn oil

8 oz/225 g skinless, boneless turkey
   breast, trimmed of all visible fat and
   cut into thin strips

2 cups snow peas

4 oz/115 g oyster mushrooms,
   torn into pieces

1/4 cup shelled pistachio nuts,
   finely chopped

2 tbsp chopped fresh cilantro

1 tbsp snipped fresh garlic chives

salt and pepper

1 tbsp balsamic vinegar

fresh garlic chives, to garnish

Set aside 3 tablespoons of the chicken stock and bring the remainder to a boil in a large pan. Add the rice and cook for 30 minutes, or until tender. Drain and let cool slightly.

Meanwhile, heat 1 tablespoon of the oil in a preheated wok or skillet. Stir-fry the turkey over medium heat for 3–4 minutes, or until cooked through. Using a slotted spoon, transfer the turkey to a dish. Add the snow peas and mushrooms to the wok and stir-fry for 1 minute. Add the reserved stock, bring to a boil, then reduce the heat, cover, and let simmer for 3–4 minutes. Transfer the vegetables to the dish and let cool slightly.

Thoroughly mix the rice, turkey, snow peas, mushrooms, nuts, cilantro, and garlic chives together, then season to taste with salt and pepper. Drizzle with the remaining corn oil and the vinegar and garnish with fresh garlic chives. Serve warm.

smoked chicken & cranberry salad

serves 4

ingredients

1 smoked chicken, weighing 3 lb/1.3 kg

scant 1 cup dried cranberries

2 tbsp apple juice or water

7 oz/200 g sugar snap peas

2 ripe avocados

juice of ½ lemon

4 lettuce hearts

1 bunch watercress, trimmed

2 oz/55 g arugula

for the dressing

2 tbsp olive oil

1 tbsp walnut oil

2 tbsp lemon juice

1 tbsp chopped fresh mixed herbs,
    such as parsley and lemon thyme

salt and pepper

Carve the chicken carefully, slicing the white meat. Divide the legs into thighs and drumsticks and trim the wings. Cover with plastic wrap and refrigerate.

Put the cranberries in a bowl. Stir in the apple juice, then cover with plastic wrap and let soak for 30 minutes.

Meanwhile, blanch the sugar snap peas, then refresh under cold running water and drain.

Peel, pit and slice the avocados and toss in the lemon juice to prevent discoloration.

Separate the lettuce hearts and arrange on a large serving platter with the avocados, sugar snap peas, watercress, arugula, and the chicken.

Put all the dressing ingredients, with salt and pepper to taste, in a screw-top jar, then screw on the lid and shake until well blended.

Drain the cranberries and mix them with the dressing, then pour over the salad. Serve immediately.

melon, chorizo & artichoke salad

serves 8

ingredients

12 small globe artichokes

juice of ½ lemon

2 tbsp Spanish olive oil

1 small orange-fleshed melon,
   such as cantaloupe

7 oz/200 g chorizo sausage,
   outer casing removed

fresh tarragon or flat-leaf parsley sprigs,
   to garnish

for the dressing

3 tbsp Spanish extra-virgin olive oil

1 tbsp red wine vinegar

1 tsp prepared mustard

1 tbsp chopped fresh tarragon

salt and pepper

Prepare the artichokes then brush the cut surfaces of the artichokes with lemon juice to prevent discoloration. Carefully remove the choke (the mass of silky hairs) by pulling it out with your fingers or by scooping it out with a spoon. It is very important to remove all the choke on older artichokes, as the little barbs, if eaten, can irritate the throat. Cut the artichokes into fourths and brush them again with lemon juice.

Heat the olive oil in a large, heavy-bottom skillet. Add the prepared artichokes and cook, stirring frequently, for 5 minutes, or until the artichoke leaves are golden brown. Remove from the skillet, then transfer to a large serving bowl and let cool.

To prepare the melon, cut in half and scoop out the seeds with a spoon. Cut the flesh into bite-size cubes. Add to the cooled artichokes. Cut the chorizo into bite-size chunks and add to the melon and artichokes.

To make the dressing, place all the ingredients in a small bowl and whisk together. Just before serving, pour the dressing over the prepared salad ingredients and toss together. Serve the salad garnished with tarragon or parsley sprigs.

layered chicken salad

serves 4

ingredients

1 lb 10 oz/750 g new potatoes, scrubbed

1 red bell pepper, halved and seeded

1 green bell pepper, halved and seeded

2 small zucchini, sliced

1 small onion, thinly sliced

3 tomatoes, sliced

12 oz/350 g cooked chicken, sliced

chopped fresh chives, to garnish

for the dressing

⅔ cup plain yogurt

3 tbsp mayonnaise

1 tbsp chopped fresh chives

salt and pepper

Put the potatoes into a large pan, add just enough cold water to cover, and bring to a boil. Lower the heat, cover, and simmer for 15–20 minutes until tender. Meanwhile, place the bell pepper halves, skin side up, under a preheated hot broiler and broil until the skins blacken and begin to char.

Remove the bell peppers with tongs, place in a bowl, and cover with plastic wrap. Set aside until cool enough to handle, then peel off the skins and slice the flesh.

Bring a small pan of lightly salted water to a boil. Add the zucchini, bring back to a boil, and simmer for 3 minutes. Drain, rinse under cold running water to prevent any further cooking, and drain again. Set aside.

To make the dressing, whisk the yogurt, mayonnaise, and chopped chives together in a small bowl until well blended. Season to taste with salt and pepper.

When the potatoes are tender, drain, cool, and slice them. Add them to the dressing and mix gently to coat evenly. Spoon the potatoes onto 4 serving plates, dividing them equally.

Top each plate with one quarter of the bell pepper slices and zucchini. Layer one quarter of the onion and tomato slices, then the sliced chicken, on top of each serving. Garnish with chopped chives and serve immediately.

rare roast beef pasta salad

serves 4

ingredients

1 lb/450 g round or sirloin steak
    in a single piece
salt and pepper
4 cups dried fusilli
4 tbsp olive oil
2 tbsp lime juice
2 tbsp Thai fish sauce
2 tsp honey
4 scallions, sliced
1 cucumber, peeled and cut into
    1-inch/2.5-cm chunks
3 tomatoes, cut into wedges
1 tbsp finely chopped fresh mint

Season the steak with salt and pepper. Broil or pan-fry it for 4 minutes on each side. Let rest for 5 minutes, then slice thinly across the grain.

Meanwhile, bring a large pan of lightly salted water to a boil. Add the pasta, bring back to a boil, and cook for 8–10 minutes or until tender, but still firm to the bite. Drain the fusilli, refresh in cold water, and drain again thoroughly. Toss the fusilli in the olive oil and set aside until required.

Combine the lime juice, fish sauce, and honey in a small pan and cook over medium heat for 2 minutes.

Add the scallions, cucumber, tomatoes, and mint to the pan, then add the steak and mix well. Season to taste with salt.

Transfer the fusilli to a large, warm serving dish and top with the steak and salad mixture. Serve just warm or let cool completely.

roast duck salad

serves 4

ingredients

2 duck breasts

2 Boston lettuces, shredded

1 cup bean sprouts

1 yellow bell pepper, seeded and
   cut into thin strips

½ cucumber, seeded and
   cut into short thin sticks

2 tsp shredded lime zest

2 tbsp shredded coconut, toasted

for the dressing

juice of 2 limes

3 tbsp fish sauce

1 tbsp soft brown sugar

2 tsp sweet chili sauce

1 inch/2.5 cm fresh gingerroot,
   grated finely

3 tbsp chopped fresh mint

3 tbsp chopped fresh basil

Preheat the oven to 400°F/200°C. Place the duck breasts on a rack set over a roasting pan and roast in the oven for 20–30 minutes, or until cooked as desired and the skin is crisp. Remove from the oven and set aside to cool.

In a large bowl, combine the lettuce, bean sprouts, bell pepper and cucumber. Cut the cooled duck into slices and add to the salad. Mix well.

In a bowl, whisk together the lime juice, fish sauce, sugar, chili sauce, gingerroot, mint, and basil. Add the dressing to the salad and toss well.

Turn the salad out onto a serving platter and garnish with the lime zest and shredded coconut before serving.

warm mushroom, spinach, & pancetta salad

serves 4

ingredients

generous 6 cups fresh baby spinach leaves

2 tbsp olive oil

5½ oz/150 g pancetta

10 oz/280 g mixed wild mushrooms, sliced

for the dressing

5 tbsp olive oil

1 tbsp balsamic vinegar

1 tsp Dijon mustard

pinch of sugar

salt and pepper

To make the dressing, place the olive oil, vinegar, mustard, sugar, salt, and pepper in a small bowl and whisk together. Rinse the baby spinach under cold running water, then drain and place in a large salad bowl.

Heat the oil in a large skillet. Add the pancetta and cook for 3 minutes. Add the mushrooms and cook for 3–4 minutes, or until tender.

Pour the dressing into the skillet and immediately turn the cooked mixture and dressing into the bowl with the spinach. Toss until coated with the dressing and serve at once.

crispy spinach & bacon

serves 4

ingredients

4 tbsp olive oil

4 strips of lean bacon, diced

1 thick slice of white bread,
    crusts removed, cut into cubes

1 lb/450 g fresh spinach, torn or shredded

Heat 2 tablespoons of the olive oil over high heat in a large skillet. Add the diced bacon to the skillet and cook for 3–4 minutes, or until crisp. Remove with a slotted spoon, draining carefully, and set aside.

Toss the cubes of bread in the fat remaining in the skillet over high heat for about 4 minutes, or until crisp and golden. Remove the croutons with a slotted spoon, draining carefully, and set them aside.

Add the remaining oil to the skillet and heat. Toss the spinach in the oil over high heat for about 3 minutes, or until it has just wilted. Turn into a serving bowl and sprinkle with the bacon and croutons. Serve immediately.

thai-style chicken salad

serves 4

ingredients

14 oz/400 g small new potatoes,
    scrubbed and cut in half, lengthwise

7 oz/200 g baby corn cobs

$1\frac{1}{2}$ cups bean sprouts

3 scallions, trimmed and sliced

4 cooked, skinless chicken breasts, sliced

1 tbsp chopped lemongrass

2 tbsp chopped fresh cilantro

salt and pepper

wedges of lime, to garnish

fresh cilantro leaves, to garnish

for the dressing

6 tbsp chili oil or sesame oil

2 tbsp lime juice

1 tbsp light soy sauce

1 tbsp chopped fresh cilantro

1 small, red chile, seeded and
    finely sliced

Bring two pans of water to the boil. Put the potatoes into one pan and cook for 15 minutes until tender. Put the corn cobs into the other pan and cook for 5 minutes until tender. Drain the potatoes and corn cobs well and let cool.

When the vegetables are cool, transfer them into a large serving dish. Add the bean sprouts, scallions, chicken, lemongrass, and cilantro and season with salt and pepper.

To make the dressing, put all the ingredients into a screw-top jar and shake well. Alternatively, put them into a bowl and mix together well. Drizzle the dressing over the salad and garnish with lime wedges and cilantro leaves. Serve at once.

duck & radish salad

serves 4

ingredients

12 oz boneless duck breasts

2 tbsp all-purpose flour

salt and pepper

1 egg

2 tbsp water

2 tbsp sesame seeds

3 tbsp sesame oil

½ head Chinese cabbage, shredded

3 celery stalks, sliced finely

8 radishes, trimmed and halved

fresh basil leaves, to garnish

for the dressing

finely grated peel of 1 lime

2 tbsp lime juice

2 tbsp olive oil

1 tbsp light soy sauce

1 tbsp chopped fresh basil

salt and pepper

Put each duck breast between sheets of baking parchment or plastic wrap. Use a meat mallet or rolling pin to beat them out and flatten them slightly.

Sprinkle the flour onto a large plate and season with salt and pepper. Beat the egg and water together in a shallow bowl, then sprinkle the sesame seeds onto a separate plate.

Dip the duck breasts first into the seasoned flour, then into the egg mixture and finally into the sesame seeds, to coat the duck evenly. Heat the sesame oil in a preheated wok or large skillet.

Fry the duck breasts over a medium heat for about 8 minutes, turning once. To test whether they are cooked, insert a sharp knife into the thickest part—the juices should run clear. Lift them out and drain on paper towels.

To make the dressing for the salad, whisk together the lime peel and juice, olive oil, soy sauce, and chopped basil. Season with a little salt and pepper.

Arrange the Chinese cabbage, celery, and radish on a serving plate. Slice the duck breasts thinly and place on top of the salad. Drizzle with the dressing and garnish with fresh basil leaves. Serve at once.

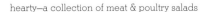

chicken, cheese & arugula salad

serves 4

ingredients

5½ oz/150 g arugula leaves

2 celery stalks, trimmed and sliced

½ cucumber, sliced

2 scallions, trimmed and sliced

2 tbsp chopped fresh parsley

1 oz/25 g walnut pieces

12 oz/350 g boneless roast chicken, sliced

4½ oz/125 g bleu cheese, cubed

handful of seedless red grapes,
   cut in half (optional)

salt and pepper

for the dressing

2 tbsp olive oil

1 tbsp sherry vinegar

1 tsp Dijon mustard

1 tbsp chopped mixed herbs

Wash the arugula leaves, pat dry with paper towels, and put them into a large salad bowl. Add the celery, cucumber, scallions, parsley, and walnuts and mix together well. Transfer onto a large serving platter. Arrange the chicken slices over the salad, then scatter over the cheese. Add the red grapes, if using. Season well with salt and pepper.

To make the dressing, put all the ingredients into a screw-top jar and shake well. Alternatively, put them into a bowl and mix together well. Drizzle the dressing over the salad and serve.

broiled lamb with
yogurt & herb dressing

serves 4

ingredients

2 tbsp sunflower oil, plus extra
    for broiling the lamb

1 tbsp tomato paste

½ tbsp ground cumin

1 tsp lemon juice

1 garlic clove, crushed

pinch of cayenne pepper

salt and pepper

1 lb 2 oz/500 g lamb neck fillets,
    trimmed with excess fat removed

toasted sesame seeds and chopped
    fresh parsley, to garnish

for the dressing

2 tbsp fresh lemon juice

1 tsp honey

3 oz/75 g thick plain yogurt

2 tbsp finely shredded fresh mint

2 tbsp chopped fresh parsley

1 tbsp finely snipped fresh chives

salt and pepper

Mix the 2 tablespoons oil, tomato paste, cumin, lemon juice, garlic, cayenne and salt and pepper to taste together in a non-metallic bowl. Add the lamb and rub all over with the marinade. Cover the bowl and marinate in the refrigerator for at least 2 hours, but ideally overnight.

Meanwhile, to make the dressing, whisk the lemon juice and honey together until the honey dissolves. Whisk in the yogurt until well blended. Stir in the herbs and add salt and pepper to taste. Cover and chill until required.

Remove the lamb from the fridge 15 minutes before you are ready to cook. Heat the broiler to its highest setting and lightly brush the broiler rack with oil. Broil the lamb, turning it once, for 10 minutes for medium and 12 minutes for well done. Leave the lamb to cool completely, then cover and chill until required.

Thinly slice the lamb, then divide among 4 plates. Adjust the seasoning in the dressing, if necessary, then spoon over the lamb slices. Sprinkle with toasted sesame seeds and parsley and serve.

smoked chicken salad with avocado & tarragon dressing

serves 4–6

ingredients

2 large, juicy tomatoes, sliced

1 lb 5 oz/600 g smoked chicken, skinned
     and cut into slices

9 oz/250 g fresh watercress, any thick
     stems or yellow leaves removed, then
     rinsed and patted dry

3 oz/75 g fresh bean sprouts, soaked for
     20 minutes in cold water, then drained
     well and patted dry

leaves from several sprigs fresh flat-leaf
     parsley or cilantro

for the dressing

1 ripe, soft avocado

2 tbsp lemon juice

1 tbsp tarragon vinegar

3 oz/75 g thick plain yogurt

1 small garlic clove, crushed

1 tbsp chopped fresh tarragon leaves

salt and pepper

To make the dressing, put the avocado, lemon juice, and vinegar in a blender or food processor and blend until smooth, scraping down the side with a rubber spatula. Add the yogurt, garlic, and tarragon leaves and process again. Season with salt and pepper to taste, then transfer to a bowl. Cover closely with plastic wrap and chill for 2 hours.

To assemble the salad, divide the tomato slices among 4–6 individual plates. Toss the smoked chicken, watercress, bean sprouts and parsley or cilantro leaves together. Divide the salad ingredients among the plates.

Adjust the seasoning in the dressing, if necessary. Spoon the dressing over each salad and serve.

roast pork & pumpkin salad

serves 4–6

ingredients

1 small pumpkin, about 3½ lb/1.6 kg

2 red onions, cut into wedges

olive oil

3½ oz/100 g green beans, topped and
    tailed and cut in half

1¼ lb/600 g roast pork, any skin or rind
    removed and cut into bite-size chunks

large handful fresh arugula leaves

3½ oz/100 g feta cheese, drained and
    crumbled

2 tbsp toasted pine nuts

2 tbsp chopped fresh parsley

salt and pepper

for the vinaigrette

6 tbsp extra-virgin olive oil

3 tbsp balsamic vinegar

½ tsp sugar

½ tsp Dijon, prepared English or
    wholegrain mustard

salt and pepper

Preheat the oven to 400°F/200°C. Cut the pumpkin in half, scoop out the seeds and fibers and cut the flesh into wedges about 1½ inches/4 cm wide. Very lightly rub the pumpkin and onion wedges with the olive oil, place in a roasting pan and roast for 25–30 minutes until the pumpkin and onions are tender but holding their shape.

Meanwhile, bring a small pan of salted water to a boil. Add the green beans and blanch for 5 minutes, or until tender. Drain well and cool under cold running water to stop the cooking. Drain well and pat dry.

Remove the pumpkin and onion wedges from the oven as soon as they are tender-crisp and leave to cool completely. When the pumpkin is cool, peel and cut into bite-size pieces.

To make the vinaigrette, put the oil, vinegar, sugar, mustard, and salt and pepper to taste into a screw-top jar and shake until blended.

To assemble the salad, put the pumpkins, onions, beans, pork, arugula, feta, pine nuts, and parsley in a large bowl and gently toss together—be careful not to break up the pumpkin. Shake the dressing again, pour over the salad and gently toss. Divide among individual bowls and serve.

roast chicken with pesto cream salad

serves 4–6

ingredients

1 lb 5 oz/600 g cooked boneless chicken,
    any skin removed and cut into
    bite-size chunks
3 celery sticks, chopped
2 large skinned red bell peppers
    from a jar, well drained and sliced
salt and pepper
iceberg lettuce leaves, to serve

for the pesto cream

5 oz/150 ml sour cream
about 4 tbsp bottled pesto sauce

To make the pesto cream, put the sour cream into a large bowl, then beat in 4 tablespoons pesto sauce. Taste and add more pesto if you want a stronger flavor.

Add the chicken, celery and bell peppers to the bowl and gently toss together. Add salt and pepper to taste and toss again. Cover and chill until required.

Remove the salad from the refrigerator 10 minutes before serving to return to room temperature. Give the salad ingredients a good stir, then divide among individual plates lined with lettuce leaves.

sparkling
a collection of fish and seafood salads

salad niçoise

serves 4

ingredients

2 tuna steaks, about ¾ inch/2 cm thick

olive oil, for brushing

salt and pepper

9 oz/250 g green beans, trimmed

½ cup vinaigrette or garlic vinaigrette
    dressing

2 hearts of lettuce, leaves separated

3 large hard-cooked eggs, cut into fourths

2 juicy vine-ripened tomatoes,
    cut into wedges

1¾ oz/50 g anchovy fillets in oil, drained

2 oz/55 g Niçoise olives, pitted

Heat a ridged cast-iron grill pan over high heat, until you can feel the heat rising from the surface. Brush the tuna steaks with oil, place oiled side down on the hot pan, and cook for 2 minutes. Lightly brush the top sides of the tuna steaks with more oil. Use a pair of tongs to turn the tuna steaks over, then season to taste with salt and pepper. Continue cooking for another 2 minutes for rare or up to 4 minutes for well done. Let cool.

Meanwhile, bring a pan of salted water to a boil. Add the beans to the pan and return to a boil, then boil for 3 minutes, or until tender-crisp. Drain the beans and immediately transfer them to a large bowl. Pour over the vinaigrette and stir together, then let the beans cool in the dressing.

To serve, line a platter with lettuce leaves. Lift the beans out of the bowl, leaving the excess dressing behind, and pile them in the center of the platter. Break the tuna into large pieces and arrange it over the beans. Arrange the hard-cooked eggs and the tomatoes around the side. Arrange the anchovy fillets over the salad, then scatter with the olives. Drizzle the remaining dressing in the bowl over everything and serve.

lentil & tuna salad

serves 4

ingredients

2 ripe tomatoes

1 small red onion

14 oz/400 g can lentils, drained

6½ oz/185 g can tuna, drained

2 tbsp chopped fresh cilantro

pepper

for the dressing

3 tbsp virgin olive oil

1 tbsp lemon juice

1 tsp whole-grain mustard

1 garlic clove, crushed

½ tsp ground cumin

½ tsp ground coriander

Using a sharp knife, seed the tomatoes and then chop them into fine dice. Finely chop the red onion.

To make the dressing, whisk together the virgin olive oil, lemon juice, mustard, garlic, cumin, and ground coriander in a small bowl until thoroughly combined. Set aside until required.

Mix together the chopped onion, diced tomatoes, and drained lentils in a large bowl.

Flake the tuna with a fork and stir it into the onion, tomato, and lentil mixture. Stir in the chopped fresh cilantro and mix well.

Pour the dressing over the lentil and tuna salad and season with pepper to taste. Serve immediately.

tuna & two-bean salad

ingredients

7 oz/200 g green beans

14 oz/400 g canned small white beans,
    such as cannellini, rinsed and drained

4 scallions, finely chopped

2 fresh tuna steaks, about 8 oz/225 g each
    and ¾ inch/2 cm thick

olive oil, for brushing

salt and pepper

9 oz/250 g cherry tomatoes, halved

lettuce leaves

fresh mint and parsley sprigs, to garnish

for the dressing

handful of fresh mint leaves, shredded

handful of fresh parsley leaves, chopped

1 garlic clove, crushed

4 tbsp extra-virgin olive oil

1 tbsp red wine vinegar

salt and pepper

First, make the dressing. Put the mint leaves, parsley leaves, garlic, olive oil, and vinegar into a screw-top jar, add salt and pepper to taste, and shake until blended. Pour into a large bowl and set aside.

Bring a pan of lightly salted water to a boil. Add the green beans and cook for 3 minutes. Add the white beans and cook for another 4 minutes until the green beans are tender-crisp and the white beans are heated through. Drain well and add to the bowl with the dressing and scallions. Toss together.

To cook the tuna, heat a stovetop ridged grill pan over high heat. Lightly brush the tuna steaks with oil, then season to taste with salt and pepper. Cook the steaks for 2 minutes, then turn over and cook on the other side for an additional 2 minutes for rare or up to 4 minutes for well done.

Remove the tuna from the grill pan and leave to rest for 2 minutes, or alternatively leave until completely cool. When ready to serve, add the tomatoes to the bean mixture and toss lightly. Line a serving platter with lettuce leaves and pile on the bean salad. Place the tuna over the top. Serve warm or at room temperature, garnished with the herbs.

tuna & fresh vegetable salad

serves 4

ingredients

12 cherry tomatoes, halved

1½ cups whole green beans,
    cut into 1-inch/2.5-cm pieces

8 oz/225 g zucchini, sliced thinly

3¼ cups thinly sliced white mushrooms

salad greens

12 oz/350 g canned tuna in brine,
    drained and flaked

fresh parsley, to garnish

for the dressing

4 tbsp mayonnaise

4 tbsp plain yogurt

2 tbsp white wine vinegar

salt and pepper

To make the dressing, put the mayonnaise, yogurt, vinegar, salt, and pepper in a screw-topped jar and shake together until the ingredients are well blended.

Put the tomatoes, beans, zucchini, and mushrooms in a bowl. Pour over the dressing and marinate for about 1 hour.

Arrange the salad leaves on a serving dish. Add the vegetables and then the tuna, and garnish with parsley.

shrimp & mango salad

serves 4

ingredients

2 mangoes

2 cups peeled, cooked shrimp

salad greens, to serve

4 whole cooked shrimp, to garnish

for the dressing

juice from the mangoes

6 tbsp plain yogurt

2 tbsp mayonnaise

1 tbsp lemon juice

salt and pepper

Cutting close to the pit, cut a large slice from one side of each mango, then cut another slice from the opposite side. Without breaking the skin, cut the flesh in the segments into squares, then push the skin inside out to expose the cubes, and cut away from the skin. Use a sharp knife to peel the remaining center section and cut the flesh away from the pit into cubes. Reserve any juice in a bowl and put the mango flesh in a separate bowl.

Add the shrimp to the mango flesh. Add the yogurt, mayonnaise, lemon juice, salt, and pepper to the juice and blend together.

Arrange the salad greens on a serving dish and add the mango flesh and shrimp. Pour the dressing over them and serve garnished with the whole shrimp.

salmon & avocado salad

serves 4

ingredients

1 lb/450 g new potatoes

4 salmon steaks, about 4 oz/115 g each

1 avocado

juice of $\frac{1}{2}$ lemon

$1\frac{1}{4}$ cups baby spinach leaves

$4\frac{1}{2}$ oz/125 g mixed small salad greens,
   including watercress

12 cherry tomatoes, halved

scant $\frac{1}{2}$ cup chopped walnuts

for the dressing

3 tbsp unsweetened clear apple juice

1 tsp balsamic vinegar

freshly ground black pepper

Cut the new potatoes into bite-size pieces, put into a pan, and cover with cold water. Bring to a boil, then reduce the heat, cover, and let simmer for 10–15 minutes, or until just tender. Drain and keep warm.

Meanwhile, preheat the broiler to medium. Cook the salmon steaks under the preheated broiler for 10–15 minutes, depending on the thickness of the steaks, turning halfway through cooking. Remove from the broiler and keep warm.

While the potatoes and salmon are cooking, cut the avocado in half, remove and discard the pit, and peel the flesh. Cut the avocado flesh into slices and coat in the lemon juice to prevent it discoloring.

Toss the spinach leaves and mixed salad greens together in a large serving bowl until combined. Arrange 6 cherry tomato halves on each plate of salad.

Remove and discard the skin and any bones from the salmon. Flake the salmon and divide among the plates along with the potatoes. Sprinkle the walnuts over the salads.

To make the dressing, mix the apple juice and vinegar together in a small bowl or pitcher and season well with pepper. Drizzle over the salads and serve at once.

coconut shrimp with cucumber salad

serves 4

ingredients

1 cup brown basmati rice

½ tsp coriander seeds

2 egg whites, lightly beaten

generous ¾ cup dry unsweetened coconut

24 raw jumbo shrimp, shelled

½ cucumber

4 scallions, thinly sliced lengthwise

1 tsp sesame oil

1 tbsp finely chopped fresh cilantro

Bring a large pan of water to a boil, add the rice, and cook for 25 minutes, or until tender. Drain and keep in a strainer covered with a clean dish towel to absorb the steam.

Meanwhile, soak 8 wooden skewers in cold water for 30 minutes, then drain. Crush the coriander seeds in a mortar with a pestle. Heat a nonstick skillet over medium heat, add the crushed coriander seeds, and cook, turning, until they start to color. Tip onto a plate and set aside.

Put the egg whites into a shallow bowl and the coconut into a separate bowl. Roll each shrimp first in the egg whites, then in the coconut. Thread onto a skewer. Repeat so that each skewer is threaded with 3 coated shrimp.

Preheat the broiler to high. Using a potato peeler, peel long strips from the cucumber to create ribbons, put into a strainer to drain, then toss with the scallions and oil in a bowl, and set aside.

Cook the shrimp under the preheated broiler for 3–4 minutes on each side, or until slightly browned.

Meanwhile, mix the rice with the toasted coriander seeds and fresh cilantro and divide this and the cucumber salad among bowls. Serve with the hot shrimp skewers.

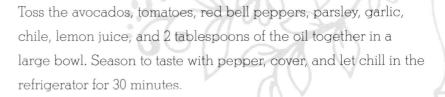

tuna & avocado salad

serves 4

ingredients

2 avocados, pitted, peeled, and cubed

9 oz/250 g cherry tomatoes, halved

2 red bell peppers, seeded and chopped

1 bunch fresh flat-leaf parsley, chopped

2 garlic cloves, crushed

1 fresh red chile, seeded and
    finely chopped

juice of $\frac{1}{2}$ lemon

6 tbsp olive oil

pepper

3 tbsp sesame seeds

4 fresh tuna steaks,
    about 5$\frac{1}{2}$ oz/150 g each

8 cooked new potatoes, cubed

arugula leaves and crusty bread, to serve

Toss the avocados, tomatoes, red bell peppers, parsley, garlic, chile, lemon juice, and 2 tablespoons of the oil together in a large bowl. Season to taste with pepper, cover, and let chill in the refrigerator for 30 minutes.

Lightly crush the sesame seeds in a mortar with a pestle. Tip the crushed seeds onto a plate and spread out. Press each tuna steak in turn into the crushed seeds to coat on both sides.

Heat 2 tablespoons of the remaining oil in a skillet, add the potatoes, and cook, stirring frequently, for 5–8 minutes, or until crisp and brown. Remove from the skillet and drain on paper towels.

Wipe out the skillet, add the remaining oil, and heat over high heat until very hot. Add the tuna steaks and cook for 3–4 minutes on each side.

To serve, divide the avocado salad among 4 serving plates. Top each with a tuna steak, sprinkle over the potatoes and arugula leaves and serve with crusty bread.

tomato, salmon & shrimp salad

serves 4

ingredients

4 oz/115 g cherry or baby plum tomatoes

several lettuce leaves

4 ripe tomatoes, coarsely chopped

3½ oz/100 g smoked salmon

7 oz/200 g large cooked shrimp,
   thawed if frozen

for the dressing

1 tbsp Dijon mustard

2 tsp superfine sugar

2 tsp red wine vinegar

2 tbsp medium olive oil

few fresh dill sprigs, plus extra to garnish

pepper

Halve most of the cherry tomatoes. Place the lettuce leaves round the edge of a shallow bowl and add all the tomatoes and cherry tomatoes. Using scissors, snip the smoked salmon into strips and sprinkle over the tomatoes, then add the shrimp.

Mix the mustard, sugar, vinegar, and oil together in a small bowl, then tear most of the dill sprigs into it. Mix well and pour over the salad. Toss well to coat the salad with the dressing. Snip the remaining dill over the top and season to taste with pepper.

lobster salad

serves 2

ingredients

2 raw lobster tails

radicchio leaves

fresh dill sprigs, to garnish

for the mayonnaise

1 large lemon

1 large egg yolk

½ tsp Dijon mustard

⅔ cup olive oil

salt and pepper

1 tbsp chopped fresh dill

To make the lemon-dill mayonnaise, finely grate half the lemon rind and squeeze the juice. Beat the egg yolk in a small bowl, then beat in the mustard and 1 teaspoon of the lemon juice.

Using a balloon whisk or electric mixer, beat the oil into the egg yolk mixture, drop by drop, until a thick mayonnaise forms. Stir in the lemon rind and 1 tablespoon of the remaining lemon juice.

Season the mayonnaise to taste with salt and pepper and add more lemon juice if desired. Stir in the dill, cover, and let chill in the refrigerator until required.

Bring a large pan of lightly salted water to a boil. Add the lobster tails, return to a boil, and cook for 6 minutes, or until the flesh is opaque and the shells are red. Drain at once and set aside to cool.

Remove the lobster flesh from the shells and cut into bite-size pieces. Arrange the radicchio leaves on individual plates and top with the lobster flesh. Place a spoonful of the lemon-dill mayonnaise on the side. Garnish with dill sprigs and serve.

russian salad

serves 4

ingredients

4 oz/115 g new potatoes

generous 1 cup frozen or shelled
   fresh fava beans

4 oz/115 g baby carrots

4 oz/115 g baby corn

4 oz/115 g baby turnips

4 oz/115 g white mushrooms,
   cut into thin sticks

12 oz/350 g cooked shelled shrimp,
   deveined

½ cup mayonnaise

1 tbsp lemon juice

2 tbsp bottled capers, drained and rinsed

salt and pepper

2 tbsp extra-virgin olive oil

2 hard-cooked eggs, shelled and halved

4 canned anchovy fillets, drained
   and halved

paprika, to garnish

Cook the new potatoes, fava beans, carrots, corn, and turnips simultaneously. Cook the potatoes in a large, heavy-bottom pan of lightly salted boiling water for 20 minutes. Cook the fava beans in a small pan of lightly salted water for 3 minutes, then drain, refresh under cold running water and set aside until required. Cook the carrots, corn, and turnips in a large, heavy-bottom pan of lightly salted boiling water for 6 minutes.

Mix the mushrooms and shrimp together in a bowl. Mix the mayonnaise and lemon juice together in a separate bowl, then fold half the mixture into the shrimp mixture. Fold in the capers and season to taste with salt and pepper.

Drain the mixed vegetables, refresh under cold running water and tip into a bowl. When the potatoes are cooked, drain, refresh under cold running water and tip into the bowl. Pop the fava beans out of their skins by pinching them between your index finger and thumb and add to the bowl. Add the olive oil and toss to coat. Divide the potatoes and vegetables between serving plates and top with the shrimp mixture. Place a hard-cooked egg half in the center of each and garnish with the halved anchovies. Dust the eggs with paprika and serve with the remaining mayonnaise mixture.

seafood salad

serves 4

ingredients

9 oz/250 g live mussels

12 oz/350 g live scallops, shucked
and cleaned

9 oz/250 g prepared squid, cut into rings
and tentacles

1 red onion, halved and finely sliced

chopped parsley, to serve

lemon wedges, to serve

for the dressing

4 tbsp extra-virgin olive oil

2 tbsp white wine vinegar

1 tbsp lemon juice

1 garlic clove, finely chopped

1 tbsp chopped fresh flat-leaf parsley

salt and pepper

Clean the mussels by scrubbing or scraping the shells and pulling out any beards that are attached to them. Discard any with broken shells or any that refuse to close when tapped. Put the mussels in a colander and rinse well under cold running water. Put them in a large pan with a little water and cook, covered, over a high heat, shaking the pan occasionally, for 3–4 minutes, or until the mussels have opened. Discard any mussels that remain closed. Strain the mussels, reserving the cooking liquid. Refresh the mussels under cold running water, drain, and set aside.

Return the reserved cooking liquid to the pan and bring to a boil, add the scallops and squid, and cook for 3 minutes. Remove from the heat and drain. Refresh under cold running water and drain again. Remove the mussels from their shells. Put them in a bowl with the scallops and squid and let cool. Cover with plastic wrap and let chill in the refrigerator for 45 minutes.

Divide the seafood among 4 serving plates and top with the onion. Combine all the dressing ingredients in a small bowl, then drizzle over the salad. Garnish with chopped parsley and lemon wedges to serve.

cantaloupe & crab salad

serves 4

ingredients

12 oz/350 g fresh crabmeat

5 tbsp mayonnaise

2 fl oz/50 ml plain yogurt

4 tsp extra-virgin olive oil

4 tsp lime juice

1 scallion, finely chopped

4 tsp finely chopped fresh parsley

pinch of cayenne pepper

1 cantaloupe melon

2 radicchio heads, separated into leaves

fresh parsley sprigs, to garnish

crusty bread, to serve

Place the crabmeat in a large bowl and pick over it very carefully to remove any remaining shell or cartilage, but try not to break up the meat.

Put the mayonnaise, yogurt, olive oil, lime juice, scallion, chopped fresh parsley, and cayenne pepper into a separate bowl and mix until thoroughly blended. Fold in the crabmeat.

Cut the melon in half and remove and discard the seeds. Slice into wedges, then cut off the rind with a sharp knife.

Arrange the melon slices and radicchio leaves on 4 large serving plates, then arrange the crabmeat mixture on top. Garnish with a few sprigs of fresh parsley and serve with fresh crusty bread.

shrimp & rice salad

serves 4

ingredients

scant 1 cup mixed long-grain and wild rice

salt and pepper

12 oz/350 g cooked shelled shrimp

1 mango, peeled, seeded, and diced

4 scallions, sliced

¼ cup slivered almonds

1 tbsp finely chopped fresh mint

for the dressing

1 tbsp extra-virgin olive oil

2 tsp lime juice

1 garlic clove, crushed

1 tsp honey

salt and pepper

Cook the rice in a large pan of lightly salted boiling water for 35 minutes, or until tender. Drain and transfer to a large bowl, then add the shrimp.

To make the dressing, mix all the ingredients together in a large measuring cup, seasoning to taste with the salt and pepper, and whisk well until thoroughly blended. Pour the dressing over the rice and shrimp mixture and let cool.

Add the mango, scallions, almonds, and mint to the salad and season to taste with pepper. Stir thoroughly, transfer to a large serving dish and serve.

anchovy & olive salad

serves 4

ingredients

large handful of mixed lettuce leaves

12 cherry tomatoes, halved

20 black olives, pitted and halved

6 canned anchovy fillets, drained
   and sliced

1 tbsp chopped fresh oregano

wedges of lemon, to garnish

crusty bread rolls, to serve

for the dressing

4 tbsp extra-virgin olive oil

1 tbsp white wine vinegar

1 tbsp lemon juice

1 tbsp chopped fresh flat-leaf parsley

salt and pepper

Prepare all the salad ingredients as per ingredients list. To make the dressing, put all the ingredients into a small bowl, seasoning with salt and pepper to taste, and stir together well.

To assemble the salad, arrange the lettuce leaves in a serving dish. Scatter the cherry tomatoes on top, followed by the olives, anchovies, and oregano. Drizzle over the dressing.

Transfer to individual plates, garnish with lemon wedges and serve with crusty bread rolls.

smoked salmon & wild arugula salad

serves 4

ingredients

1¾ oz/50 g wild arugula leaves

1 tbsp chopped fresh flat-leaf parsley

2 scallions, finely diced

2 large avocados

1 tbsp lemon juice

9 oz/250 g smoked salmon

for the dressing

⅔ cup mayonnaise

2 tbsp lime juice

finely grated rind of 1 lime

1 tbsp chopped fresh flat-leaf parsley,
    plus extra sprigs to garnish

Shred the arugula and arrange in 4 individual glass bowls.
Sprinkle over the chopped parsley and scallions.

Halve, peel, and pit the avocados and cut into thin slices or small
chunks. Brush with the lemon juice to prevent discoloration,
then divide among the salad bowls. Mix together gently. Cut the
smoked salmon into strips and sprinkle over the top.

Put the mayonnaise in a bowl, then add the lime juice, lime
rind, and chopped parsley. Mix together well. Spoon some of
the mayonnaise dressing on top of each salad and garnish with
parsley sprigs.

tuna & herbed fusilli salad

ingredients

7 oz/200 g dried fusilli

1 red bell pepper, seeded and quartered

1 red onion, sliced

4 tomatoes, sliced

7 oz/200 g canned tuna in brine,
    drained and flaked

for the dressing

6 tbsp basil-flavored oil or
    extra-virgin olive oil

3 tbsp white wine vinegar

1 tbsp lime juice

1 tsp mustard

1 tsp honey

4 tbsp chopped fresh basil, plus extra
    sprigs to garnish

Bring a large pan of lightly salted water to a boil. Add the pasta, return to a boil, and cook for 8–10 minutes until tender but still firm to the bite.

Meanwhile, put the bell pepper quarters under a preheated hot broiler and cook for 10–12 minutes until the skins begin to blacken. Transfer to a plastic bag, seal, and set aside.

Remove the pasta from the heat, drain, and set aside to cool. Remove the bell pepper quarters from the bag and peel off the skins. Slice the bell pepper into strips.

To make the dressing, put all the dressing ingredients in a large bowl and stir together well. Add the pasta, bell pepper strips, onion, tomatoes, and tuna. Toss together gently, then divide among serving bowls. Garnish with basil sprigs and serve.

seafood & spinach salad

serves 4

ingredients

1 lb 2 oz/500 g live mussels, soaked
    and cleaned

3½ oz/100 g shrimp, peeled and deveined

12 oz/350 g scallops

1 lb 2 oz/500 g baby spinach leaves

3 scallions, trimmed and sliced

for the dressing

4 tbsp extra-virgin olive oil

2 tbsp white wine vinegar

1 tbsp lemon juice

1 tsp finely grated lemon zest

1 garlic clove, chopped

1 tbsp grated fresh gingerroot

1 small red chile, seeded and diced

1 tbsp chopped fresh cilantro

salt and pepper

Put the mussels into a large pan with a little water, bring to a boil, and cook over high heat for 4 minutes. Drain and reserve the liquid. Discard any mussels that remain closed. Return the reserved liquid to the pan and bring to a boil. Add the shrimp and scallops and cook for 3 minutes. Drain. Remove the mussels from their shells. Rinse the mussels, shrimp, and scallops in cold water, drain, and put them in a large bowl. Cool, cover with plastic wrap, and chill for 45 minutes. Meanwhile, rinse the baby spinach leaves and transfer them to a pan with 4 tablespoons of water. Cook over high heat for 1 minute, transfer to a strainer, refresh under cold running water, and drain.

To make the dressing, put all the ingredients into a small bowl and mix. Arrange the spinach on serving dishes, then scatter over half of the scallions. Top with the mussels, shrimp and scallops, then scatter over the remaining scallions. Drizzle over the dressing and serve.

neapolitan seafood salad

serves 4

ingredients

1 lb/450 g prepared squid, cut into strips

1 lb 10 oz/750 g cooked mussels

1 lb 10 oz/750 g cooked cockles in brine

$\frac{5}{8}$ cup white wine

$1\frac{1}{2}$ cups olive oil

2 cups dried campanelle or other
   small pasta shapes

juice of 1 lemon

1 bunch chives, snipped

1 bunch fresh parsley, finely chopped

salt and pepper

mixed salad greens

4 large tomatoes, to garnish

Put all of the seafood into a large bowl. Pour over the wine and half the olive oil, then set aside for 6 hours.

Put the seafood mixture into a pan and simmer over a low heat for 10 minutes. Set aside to cool.

Bring a large pan of lightly salted water to a boil. Add the pasta and 1 tbsp of the remaining olive oil and cook until tender, but still firm to the bite. Drain thoroughly and refresh in cold water.

Strain off about half of the cooking liquid from the seafood and discard the rest. Mix in the lemon juice, chives, parsley, and the remaining olive oil. Season to taste with salt and pepper. Drain the pasta and add to the seafood.

Shred the leaves and arrange them at the base of a salad bowl. Cut the tomatoes into quarters. Spoon the seafood salad into the bowl, garnish with the tomatoes and serve.

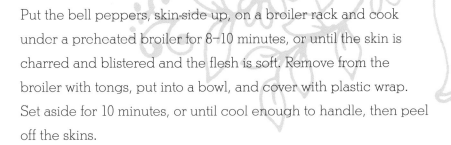

mussel salad

serves 4

ingredients

2 red bell peppers, halved and seeded

12 oz/350 g cooked, shucked mussels,
   thawed if frozen

1 head radicchio

¾ cup arugula

8 cooked green-lipped mussels in
   their shells

for the dressing

1 tbsp olive oil

1 tbsp lemon juice

1 tsp finely grated lemon peel

2 tsp honey

1 tsp French mustard

1 tbsp snipped fresh chives

salt and pepper

Put the bell peppers, skin-side up, on a broiler rack and cook under a preheated broiler for 8–10 minutes, or until the skin is charred and blistered and the flesh is soft. Remove from the broiler with tongs, put into a bowl, and cover with plastic wrap. Set aside for 10 minutes, or until cool enough to handle, then peel off the skins.

Slice the bell pepper flesh into thin strips and put into a bowl. Gently stir in the shucked mussels.

To make the dressing, whisk the oil, lemon juice and peel, honey, mustard, and chives together until well blended. Season to taste with salt and pepper. Add the bell pepper and mussel mixture and toss until coated.

Remove the central core of the radicchio and shred the leaves. Put into a serving bowl with the arugula and toss together.

Pile the mussel mixture into the center of the leaves and arrange the green-lipped mussels in their shells around the edge of the bowl.

sweet & sour fish salad

serves 4

ingredients

8 oz/225 g trout fillets

8 oz/225 g white fish fillets
   (such as haddock or cod)

1¼ cups water

1 stem lemongrass

2 lime leaves

1 large red chile

1 bunch scallions, trimmed and shredded

4 oz/115 g fresh pineapple flesh, diced

1 small red bell pepper, seeded
   and diced

1 bunch watercress, washed and trimmed

fresh snipped chives, to garnish

for the dressing

1 tbsp sunflower oil

1 tbsp rice wine vinegar

pinch of chili powder

1 tsp clear honey

salt and pepper

Rinse the fish, place in a skillet and pour over the water. Bend the lemongrass in half to bruise it and add to the skillet with the lime leaves. Prick the chile with a fork and add to the pan. Bring to a boil and simmer for 7–8 minutes. Let cool.

Drain the fish fillet thoroughly, then flake the flesh away from the skin and place it in a bowl. Gently stir in the scallions, pineapple and bell pepper.

Arrange the washed watercress on 4 serving plates and spoon the cooked fish mixture on top.

To make the dressing, mix all the ingredients together, seasoning well. Spoon it over the fish and serve the salad garnished with chives.

chiled shrimp with pineapple & papaya salsa

serves 8

ingredients

4 tbsp sunflower oil

1 fresh red chile, seeded and chopped

1 garlic clove, crushed

48 shrimps

chopped fresh parsley, to garnish

for the pineapple & papaya salsa

1 large papaya, halved, seeded, peeled
    and cut into 1/4-inch/5 mm dice

1 small pineapple, halved, cored, peeled
    and cut into 1/4 inch/5 mm dice

2 scallions, very finely chopped

1 fresh red chile, or to taste, seeded and
    finely chopped

1 garlic clove, very finely chopped

2 1/2 tsp lemon juice

1/2 tsp ground cumin

1/4 tsp salt

black pepper

To make the salsa, put the papaya in a large bowl with the pineapple, scallions, chile, garlic, lemon juice, cumin, salt and pepper. Adjust the lemon juice, cumin, salt or pepper to taste, if necessary. Cover and chill until required, ideally at least 2 hours.

Heat a wok over a high heat. Add the oil and swirl around, then add the chile and garlic and stir-fry for 20 seconds. Add the shrimp and stir-fry for 2–3 minutes until the shrimp are cooked through, become pink and curl.

Tip the shrimps, garlic and any oil left in the wok into a heatproof bowl and leave the shrimp to cool and marinate in the chile oil. When the shrimps are completely cool, cover the bowl and chill for at least 2 hours.

When ready to serve, give the salsa a stir and adjust the seasoning, if necessary. Arrange a mound of salsa on each of 8 plates. Remove the shrimp from the marinade and divide among plates. Sprinkle with parsley and serve.

seared swordfish with fresh tomato salsa

serves 4

ingredients

4 boneless swordfish steaks, about
    5 oz/140 g each

salt and pepper

stick of butter

1 tbsp olive oil

slices of crusty bread, to serve

for the fresh tomato & olive salsa

4 tbsp extra-virgin olive oil

1 tbsp red-wine vinegar

1 lb 5 oz/600 g ripe, juicy beefsteak
    tomatoes, cored, seeded and finely
    chopped

5 oz/140 g large black olives, pitted and
    cut in half

1 shallot, finely chopped or thinly sliced

1 tbsp capers in brine, rinsed and dried

salt and pepper

3 tbsp finely shredded fresh basil leaves

To make the fresh tomato & olive salsa, whisk the olive oil and vinegar together in a bowl large enough to hold all the ingredients. Gently stir in the tomatoes, olives, shallot, and capers with salt and pepper to taste. Cover and chill until required.

Season the swordfish steaks on both sides with salt. Melt the butter with the oil in a skillet large enough to hold the swordfish steaks in a single layer. (If you don't have a large enough pan, cook the steaks in 2 batches.)

Add the swordfish steaks to the pan in a single layer and fry for 5 minutes, or until golden brown, then carefully turn the fish over and continue frying about 3 minutes longer until the fish is cooked through and flakes easily. Remove the fish from the pan and set aside to cool completely. Cover and chill for at least 2 hours.

When ready to serve, remove the fish from the fridge at least 15 minutes in advance. Stir the basil into the salsa, then adjust the seasoning if necessary. Break the swordfish into large flakes and gently stir into the salsa—take care not to break up the fish too much. Arrange the fish salad in 4 bowls, spooning over any of the left-over juices and serve with slices of crusty bread.

shrimp cocktail salad

serves 4

ingredients

2 tsp salt

½ lemon, sliced

32 large shelled and deveined shrimp,
    defrosted if frozen

6 oz/175 g tomato ketchup

1½ tbsp grated horseradish

3 celery sticks, cut into ¼-inch/
    5-mm slices

finely grated zest and juice of 1 lemon

salt and pepper

iceberg lettuce leaves, shredded, to serve

lemon wedges, to garnish

Bring a large pan of water to a rolling boil. Stir in the salt and
lemon slices, then reduce the heat to low. Add the shrimp
and leave to simmer for about 3 minutes until they are cooked
through, turn pink and curl. Drain the shrimp into a large
colander and immediately refresh under cold running water to
stop the cooking and cool the shrimps; set aside.

Put the ketchup, horseradish, celery and lemon zest in a bowl
and stir together. Stir in 1 tablespoon lemon juice, then add more
juice and salt and pepper to taste. Stir in the shrimp, then cover
and chill for at least 2 hours.

When ready to serve, stir the shrimp salad and adjust the
seasoning, if necessary. Divide the shredded lettuce among
4 glass bowls and spoon the salad on top. Serve at once while
the salad is still chilled, with lemon wedges for squeezing over.

celeriac rémoulade with crab

serves 4

ingredients

1 lb/450 g celery root, peeled and grated

juice of 1 lemon

9 oz/350 g fresh white crabmeat,
    picked over

chopped fresh dill or parsley, to garnish

for the rémoulade dressing

5 oz/150 ml mayonnaise

1 tbsp Dijon mustard

1½ tsp white wine vinegar

2 tbsp capers in brine, well rinsed

salt and white pepper

To make the dressing, put the mayonnaise in a bowl. Beat in the mustard, vinegar, and capers, with salt and white pepper to taste—the mixture should be piquant with a strong mustard flavor. Cover and chill until required.

Bring a large pan of salted water to a full, rolling boil. Meanwhile, peel the celery root and cut it into quarters, then grate it either in a food processor or on the coarse side of a box grater.

Add the grated celery root and lemon juice to the water and blanch for 1½–2 minutes until it is just slightly tender. Rinse the celery root well, then put it under cold running water to stop the cooking. Use your hands to squeeze out the excess moisture, then pat the celery root dry with paper towels or a clean kitchen towel.

Stir the celery root into the dressing, along with the crabmeat. Taste and adjust the seasoning, if necessary. Cover and chill for at least 30 minutes.

When ready to serve, spoon into bowls and sprinkle with dill or parsley.

health-boosting

a collection of energizing salads

wild rice salad with cucumber & orange

serves 4

ingredients

1⅓ cups wild rice

3½ cups water

1 each red, yellow, and orange bell
    peppers, skinned, seeded,
    and thinly sliced

½ cucumber, halved lengthwise and sliced

1 orange, peeled, pith removed, and cubed

3 ripe tomatoes, cut into chunks

1 red onion, very finely chopped

generous handful of chopped
    flat-leaf parsley

for the dressing

1 clove garlic, crushed

1 tbsp balsamic vinegar

2 tbsp extra-virgin olive oil

salt and pepper

Put the wild rice and water into a large pan and bring to a boil. Stir, then cover and simmer for 40 minutes, or until the rice is al dente (firm to the bite). Uncover the rice for the last few minutes of cooking to let any excess water evaporate.

To make the dressing, put the crushed garlic, vinegar, olive oil, and seasoning into a screw-top jar and shake vigorously. Add extra vinegar, oil, or seasoning as required.

Drain the rice and turn into a large bowl. Pour over the dressing and mix in. Then mix in the chopped bell peppers, cucumber, orange, tomatoes, red onion, and flat-leaf parsley and serve.

red bell pepper & radicchio salad

serves 4

ingredients

2 red bell peppers

1 head radicchio, separated into leaves

4 cooked whole beets, cut into matchsticks

12 radishes, sliced

4 scallions, finely chopped

4 tbsp vinaigrette

crusty bread, to serve

Core and seed the bell peppers and cut into rounds.

Arrange the radicchio leaves in a salad bowl. Add the bell pepper, beets, radishes, and scallions. Drizzle with the vinaigrette and serve with crusty bread.

spring clean salad

serves 4

ingredients

2 dessert apples, cored and diced

juice of 1 lemon

large chunk of watermelon,
    seeded and cubed

1 head Belgian endive, sliced into rounds

4 sticks celery with leaves,
    coarsely chopped

1 tbsp walnut oil

Core and dice the apples. Place in a bowl and pour over the lemon juice. Mix well to prevent discoloration.

Add the rest of the fruit and vegetables to the bowl and mix gently. Pour in the walnut oil, mix again and serve.

chickpea & tomato salad

serves 4

ingredients

6 oz/175 g dried chickpeas or
   1½ cups canned, drained and rinsed
2–3 ripe tomatoes, coarsely chopped
1 red onion, thinly sliced
handful of fresh basil leaves, torn
1 romaine lettuce, torn
crusty bread, to serve

for the dressing

1 green chile, seeded and finely chopped
1 garlic clove, crushed
juice and zest of 2 lemons
2 tbsp olive oil
1 tbsp water
black pepper

If using dried chickpeas, soak overnight, then boil for 30 minutes, or until soft. Let cool.

Put the chile, garlic, lemon juice, olive oil, water, and black pepper in a screw-top jar and shake vigorously. Taste and add more lemon juice or oil if necessary.

Add the tomatoes, onion, and basil to the chickpeas and mix gently. Pour over the dressing and mix again. Arrange on a bed of lettuce and serve with crusty bread.

fennel & orange salad

serves 4

ingredients

2 oranges, peeled and sliced

1 bulb Florence fennel, thinly sliced

1 red onion, peeled and sliced
   into thin rings

for the dressing

juice of 1 orange

2 tbsp balsamic vinegar

Arrange the orange slices in the bottom of a shallow dish. Place a layer of fennel on top and then add a layer of onion.

Mix the orange juice with the vinegar and drizzle over the salad.

warm new potato & lentil salad

serves 4

ingredients

³⁄₈ cup puy lentils

1 lb/450 g new potatoes

6 scallions

1 tbsp olive oil

2 tbsp balsamic vinegar

salt and pepper

Bring a large pan of water to a boil. Rinse the lentils, then cook for 20 minutes, or until tender. Drain and rinse, then put to one side.

Meanwhile, steam or boil the potatoes until they are soft right through. Drain and halve.

Trim the base from the scallions and cut them in long strips.

Put the lentils, potatoes, and scallions into a serving dish and toss with the olive oil and vinegar. Season with plenty of black pepper and a little salt if required.

bean sprout, apricot, & almond salad

serves 4

ingredients

1²⁄₃ cups bean sprouts, washed and dried

small bunch seedless black and
    green grapes, halved

12 unsulfured dried apricots, halved

¼ cup blanched almonds, halved

black pepper

for the dressing

1 tbsp walnut oil

1 tsp sesame oil

2 tsp balsamic vinegar

Place the bean sprouts in the bottom of a large salad bowl and sprinkle the grapes and apricots on top.

Place the oils and vinegar in a screw-top jar and shake vigorously to mix. Pour over the salad.

Scatter over the almonds and season with freshly ground black pepper.

asparagus & tomato salad

serves 4

ingredients

8 oz/225 g asparagus spears

1 lamb's lettuce, washed and torn

1 handful arugula or mizuna leaves

1 lb/450 g ripe tomatoes, sliced

12 black olives, pitted and chopped

1 tbsp toasted pine nuts

for the dressing

1 tsp lemon oil

1 tbsp olive oil

1 tsp whole-grain mustard

2 tbsp balsamic vinegar

salt and pepper

Steam the asparagus spears for 8 minutes, or until tender. Rinse under cold running water to prevent them cooking any further, then cut into 2-inch/5-cm pieces.

Arrange the lettuce and arugula or mizuna leaves around a salad platter to form the base of the salad. Place the sliced tomatoes in a circle on top and the asparagus in the center.

Sprinkle the black olives and pine nuts over the top. Put the lemon oil, olive oil, mustard, and vinegar in a screw-top jar and season to taste with sea salt and black pepper. Shake vigorously and drizzle over the salad.

avocado salad

serves 4

ingredients

large handful of radicchio

large handful of arugula

1 small galia melon

2 ripe avocados

1 tbsp lemon juice

7 oz/200 g fontina cheese,
    cut into bite-size pieces

for the dressing

5 tbsp lemon-flavored or
    extra-virgin olive oil

1 tbsp white wine vinegar

1 tbsp lemon juice

1 tbsp chopped fresh parsley

To make the dressing, mix together the oil, vinegar, lemon juice, and parsley in a small bowl.

Arrange the radicchio and arugula on serving plates. Cut the melon in half, then seed it, and cut the flesh away from the skin. Discard the skin. Slice the melon flesh and arrange it over the salad greens.

Cut the avocados in half and remove and discard the pits and skin. Slice the flesh and brush with lemon juice. Arrange the slices over the melon, then scatter over the cheese. Drizzle over the dressing and serve.

herby potato salad

serves 4–6

ingredients

1 lb 2 oz/500 g new potatoes

salt and pepper

16 vine-ripened cherry tomatoes, halved

generous ⅜ cup black olives, pitted and
    coarsely chopped

4 scallions, finely sliced

2 tbsp chopped fresh mint

2 tbsp chopped fresh parsley

2 tbsp chopped fresh cilantro

juice of 1 lemon

3 tbsp extra-virgin olive oil

Cook the potatoes in a pan of lightly salted boiling water for
15 minutes, or until tender. Drain, then let cool slightly before
peeling off the skins. Cut into halves or fourths, depending on
the size of the potato. Then combine with the tomatoes, olives,
scallions, and herbs in a salad bowl.

Mix the lemon juice and oil together in a small bowl or pitcher
and pour over the potato salad. Season to taste with salt and
pepper before serving.

tabbouleh

serves 4

ingredients

generous 1 cup quinoa

2½ cups water

10 vine-ripened cherry tomatoes, seeded
 and halved

3-inch/7.5-cm piece cucumber, diced

3 scallions, finely chopped

juice of ½ lemon

2 tbsp extra-virgin olive oil

4 tbsp chopped fresh mint

4 tbsp chopped fresh cilantro

4 tbsp chopped fresh parsley

salt and pepper

Put the quinoa into a medium-size pan and cover with the water. Bring to a boil, then reduce the heat, cover, and let simmer over low heat for 15 minutes. Drain if necessary.

Let the quinoa cool slightly before combining with the remaining ingredients in a salad bowl. Adjust the seasoning, if necessary, before serving.

buckwheat noodle salad with smoked tofu

serves 2

ingredients

7 oz/200 g buckwheat noodles

9 oz/250 g firm smoked tofu
    (drained weight)

7 oz/200 g white cabbage, finely shredded

9 oz/250 g carrots, finely shredded

3 scallions, diagonally sliced

1 fresh red chile, seeded and
    finely sliced into circles

2 tbsp sesame seeds, lightly toasted

for the dressing

1 tsp grated fresh gingerroot

1 garlic clove, crushed

6 oz/175 g silken tofu (drained weight)

4 tsp tamari (wheat-free soy sauce)

2 tbsp sesame oil

4 tbsp hot water

salt

Cook the noodles in a large pan of lightly salted boiling water according to the package instructions. Drain and refresh under cold running water.

To make the dressing, blend the gingerroot, garlic, silken tofu, tamari, oil, and water together in a small bowl until smooth and creamy. Season to taste with salt.

Place the smoked tofu in a steamer. Steam for 5 minutes, then cut into thin slices.

Meanwhile, put the cabbage, carrots, scallions, and chile into a bowl and toss to mix. To serve, arrange the noodles on serving plates and top with the carrot salad and slices of tofu. Spoon over the dressing and sprinkle with sesame seeds.

zucchini & mint salad

serves 4

ingredients

2 zucchini, cut into thin sticks

3½ oz/100 g green beans, cut into thirds

1 green bell pepper, seeded and
　　cut into strips

2 celery stalks, sliced

1 bunch of watercress

for the dressing

scant 1 cup plain yogurt

1 garlic clove, crushed

2 tbsp chopped fresh mint

pepper

Cook the thin zucchini sticks and beans in a pan of lightly salted water for 7–8 minutes. Drain, rinse under cold running water, and drain again. Let cool completely.

Mix the zucchini and beans with the green bell pepper strips, celery, and watercress in a large serving bowl.

To make the dressing, combine the yogurt, garlic, and mint in a small bowl. Season to taste with pepper.

Spoon the dressing onto the salad and serve immediately.

tomato, mozzarella & avocado salad

serves 4

ingredients

2 ripe beefsteak tomatoes

3½ oz/100 g mozzarella cheese

2 avocados

few fresh basil leaves, torn into pieces

20 black olives

fresh crusty bread, to serve

for the dressing

1 tbsp olive oil

1½ tbsp white wine vinegar

1 tsp coarse grain mustard

salt and pepper

Using a sharp knife, cut the tomatoes into thick wedges and place in a large serving dish. Drain the mozzarella cheese and coarsely tear into pieces. Cut the avocados in half and remove the pits. Cut the flesh into slices, then arrange the mozzarella cheese and avocado with the tomatoes.

Mix the oil, vinegar, and mustard together in a small bowl, add salt and pepper to taste, then drizzle over the salad.

Sprinkle the basil and olives over the top and serve at once with fresh crusty bread.

roasted vegetable salad

serves 4

ingredients

1 onion

1 eggplant, about 8 oz/225 g

1 red bell pepper, seeded

1 orange bell pepper, seeded

1 large zucchini, about 6 oz/175 g

2–4 garlic cloves

2–4 tbsp olive oil

salt and pepper

1 tbsp shredded fresh basil

freshly shaved Parmesan cheese, to serve

fresh crusty bread, to serve

for the dressing

1 tbsp balsamic vinegar

2 tbsp extra-virgin olive oil

salt and pepper

Preheat the oven to 400°F/200°C. Cut all the vegetables into even-size wedges, put into a roasting pan, and sprinkle over the garlic.

Pour over 2 tablespoons of the olive oil and turn the vegetables in the oil until well coated. Add a little salt and pepper. Roast in the preheated oven for 40 minutes, or until tender, adding the extra olive oil if becoming too dry.

Meanwhile, put the vinegar, extra-virgin olive oil, and salt and pepper to taste into a screw-top jar and shake until blended.

Once the vegetables are cooked, remove from the oven, arrange on a serving dish, and pour over the dressing. Sprinkle with the basil and serve with shavings of Parmesan cheese. Serve warm or cold with fresh crusty bread.

three bean salad

serves 4–6

ingredients

6 oz/175 g mixed salad greens, such as
  spinach, arugula, and frisée

1 red onion

3 oz/85 g radishes

6 oz/175 g cherry tomatoes

4 oz/115 g cooked beet

10 oz/280 g canned cannellini beans,
  drained and rinsed

7 oz/200 g canned red kidney beans,
  drained and rinsed

10½ oz/300 g canned flageolets,
  drained and rinsed

scant ⅓ cup dried cranberries

scant ½ cup roasted cashews

8 oz/225 g feta cheese (drained weight),
  crumbled

for the dressing

4 tbsp extra-virgin olive oil

1 tsp Dijon mustard

2 tbsp lemon juice

1 tbsp chopped fresh cilantro

salt and pepper

Arrange the salad greens in a salad bowl and set aside.

Thinly slice the onion, then cut in half to form half moons and put into a bowl.

Thinly slice the radishes, cut the tomatoes in half, and peel the beet, if necessary, and dice. Add to the onion with the remaining ingredients, except the nuts and cheese.

Put all the ingredients for the dressing into a screw-top jar and shake until blended. Pour over the bean mixture, toss lightly, then spoon on top of the salad greens.

Sprinkle over the nuts and cheese and serve at once.

succatash salad

ingredients

1 tbsp apple-cider vinegar

1 tsp wholegrain mustard

1 tsp sugar

3 tbsp garlic-flavored olive oil

1 tbsp sunflower oil

14 oz/400 g canned corn kernels, rinsed
    and drained

14 oz/400 g string beans, finely chopped

2 peeled red bell peppers from a jar,
    drained and finely chopped

2 scallions, very finely chopped

salt and pepper

2 tbsp chopped fresh parsley, to garnish

Beat the vinegar, mustard and sugar together. Gradually whisk in the olive and sunflower oils to form an emulsion.

Stir in the corn kernels, string beans, bell peppers and scallions. Add salt and pepper to taste and stir together again. Cover and chill for up to one day until required.

When ready to serve, adjust the seasoning, if necessary, and stir in the parsley.

spinach salad with bleu cheese dressing

serves 4–6

ingredients

10 oz/300 g bag baby spinach leaves,
    any thick stems or yellow leaves
    removed, then well rinsed and dried
4 scallions, chopped
3 oranges, segmented
2 oz/55 g sunflower seeds

for the bleu cheese dressing

4 oz/125 g full-flavored bleu cheese,
    such as Roquefort, crumbled
7 oz/200 g thick plain yogurt
1 tbsp white wine vinegar
½ onion, grated
½ small bunch fresh chives, chopped
salt and pepper

To make the dressing, put the bleu cheese, yogurt, vinegar and onion in a blender or food processor and blend until smooth. Add the chives and give another quick blitz. Season with salt and pepper to taste. Cover and chill until required.

When you are ready to assemble the salad, place the spinach leaves and scallions in a salad bowl and toss with half the dressing. Transfer to a serving bowl and top with the orange segments and a sprinkling of sunflower seeds.

Pass the remaining dressing separately for spooning over individual portions, if desired.

pear & roquefort salad

serves 4

ingredients
few leaves of lollo rosso
few leaves of radicchio
few leaves of mâche
2 ripe pears
pepper
whole fresh chives, to garnish

for the dressing
2 oz/55 g Roquefort cheese
⅔ cup plain yogurt
2 tbsp chopped fresh chives
pepper

Place the cheese in a bowl and mash with a fork. Gradually blend the yogurt into the cheese to make a smooth dressing. Add the chives and season with pepper to taste.

Tear the lollo rosso, radicchio, and mâche leaves into manageable pieces. Arrange the salad greens on a large serving platter or divide them among individual serving plates.

Cut the pears into fourths and remove the cores. Cut the quarters into slices. Arrange the pear slices over the salad leaves.

Drizzle the dressing over the pears and garnish with a few whole chives.

green fruit salad

serves 4

ingredients

1 honeydew melon

2 green apples

2 kiwi fruit

4 oz/115 g seedless white grapes

fresh mint sprigs, to decorate

for the syrup dressing

1 orange

⅔ cup white wine

⅔ cup water

4 tbsp honey

fresh mint sprigs

To make the syrup, pare the rind from the orange using a potato peeler.

Put the orange rind in a pan with the white wine, water, and honey. Bring to a boil, then simmer gently for 10 minutes.

Remove the syrup from the heat. Add the mint sprigs and set aside to cool.

To prepare the fruit, first cut the melon in half and scoop out the seeds. Use a melon baller or a teaspoon to make melon balls.

Core and chop the apples. Peel and slice the kiwi fruit.

Strain the cooled syrup into a serving bowl, removing and reserving the orange rind, and discarding the mint sprigs.

Add the apple, grapes, kiwi fruit, and melon to the serving bowl. Stir through gently to mix.

Serve the fruit salad, decorated with sprigs of fresh mint and some of the reserved orange rind.

tropical fruit salad

serves 4

ingredients

1 papaya

1 mango

1 pineapple

4 oranges, peeled and cut into segments

4½ oz/125 g strawberries, hulled
   and quartered

light or heavy cream, to serve (optional)

for the syrup dressing

6 tbsp superfine sugar

1¾ cups water

½ tsp ground allspice

grated rind of ½ lemon

Put the sugar, water, allspice, and lemon rind into a pan. Bring to a boil, stirring continuously, then continue to boil for 1 minute. Remove from the heat and let cool to room temperature. Transfer to a pitcher or bowl, cover with plastic wrap, and chill in the refrigerator for at least 1 hour.

Peel and halve the papaya and remove the seeds. Cut the flesh into small chunks or slices, and put into a large bowl. Cut the mango twice lengthwise, close to the stone. Remove and discard the stone. Peel and cut the flesh into small chunks or slices, and add to the bowl. Cut off the top and bottom of the pineapple and remove the hard skin. Cut the pineapple in half lengthwise, then into quarters, and remove the tough core. Cut the remaining flesh into small pieces and add to the bowl. Add the orange segments and strawberries.

Pour over the chilled syrup, cover with plastic wrap, and chill until required. Serve with light or heavy cream, if using.

fig & watermelon salad

serves 4

ingredients

1 watermelon, weighing about
    3 lb 5 oz/1.5 kg

¾ cup seeded black grapes

4 figs

for the syrup dressing

1 lime

grated rind and juice of 1 orange

1 tbsp maple syrup

2 tbsp honey

Cut the watermelon into quarters and scoop out and discard the seeds. Cut the flesh away from the rind, then chop the flesh into 1 inch/2.5-cm cubes. Place the watermelon cubes in a bowl with the grapes. Cut each fig lengthwise into 8 wedges and add to the bowl.

Grate the lime rind and mix it with the orange rind and juice, maple syrup, and honey in a small pan. Bring to a boil over low heat. Pour the mixture over the fruit and stir. Let cool. Stir again, cover, and let chill in the refrigerator for at least 1 hour, stirring occasionally.

Divide the fruit salad equally among 4 bowls, and serve.

melon & mango salad

serves 4

ingredients

1 cantaloupe melon

2 oz/55 g black grapes, halved and seeded

2 oz/55 g green grapes

1 large mango

1 bunch watercress, trimmed

iceberg lettuce leaves, shredded

1 passion fruit

for the melon dressing

⅔ cup plain yogurt

1 tbsp honey

1 tsp grated fresh gingerroot

for the salad greens dressing

2 tbsp olive oil

1 tbsp apple vinegar

salt and pepper

To make the dressing for the melon, whisk together the yogurt, honey, and gingerroot in a small bowl.

Halve the melon, scoop out the seeds with a spoon, and discard. Slice, peel, and dice the flesh. Place in a bowl with the grapes.

Slice the mango on each side of its large flat pit. On each mango half, slash the flesh into a criss-cross pattern, down to but not through the skin. Push the skin from underneath to turn the mango halves inside out. Now remove the flesh and add to the melon mixture.

Arrange the watercress and lettuce leaves on 4 serving plates.

Make the dressing for the salad greens by whisking together the olive oil and vinegar with a little salt and pepper. Drizzle over the salad greens.

Divide the melon mixture among the 4 plates and spoon the yogurt dressing over it.

Scoop the seeds out of the passion fruit and sprinkle them over the salads. Serve immediately or chill in the refrigerator until required.

papaya salad

serves 4

ingredients

1 crisp lettuce

¼ small white cabbage

2 papayas

2 tomatoes

1 oz/25 g roasted peanuts, chopped
   roughly

4 scallions, trimmed and sliced thinly

basil leaves, to garnish

for the dressing

4 tbsp olive oil

1 tbsp fish sauce or light soy sauce

2 tbsp lime or lemon juice

1 tbsp dark brown sugar

1 tsp finely chopped fresh red or
   green chile

To make the dressing, whisk together the oil, fish sauce or soy sauce, lime or lemon juice, sugar and chile. Set aside, stirring occasionally to dissolve the sugar.

Shred the lettuce and white cabbage, then toss together and arrange on a large serving plate.

Peel the papayas and slice them in half. Scoop out the seeds, then slice the flesh thinly. Arrange on top of the lettuce and cabbage.

Soak the tomatoes in a bowl of boiling water for 1 minute, then lift out and peel. Remove the seeds and slice the flesh. Arrange on the salad greens.

Scatter the peanuts and scallions over the top. Whisk the dressing and pour over the salad. Garnish with basil leaves and serve at once.

exotic fruit cocktail

serves 4

ingredients

2 oranges

2 large passion fruit

1 pineapple

1 pomegranate

1 banana

Cut 1 orange in half and squeeze the juice into a bowl, discarding any pips. Using a sharp knife, cut away all the peel and pith from the second orange. Working over the bowl to catch the juice, carefully cut the orange segments between the membranes to obtain skinless segments of fruit. Discard any pips.

Cut the passion fruit in half, scoop the flesh into a nylon strainer and, using a spoon, push the pulp and juice into the bowl of orange segments. Discard the pips.

Using a sharp knife, cut away all the skin from the pineapple and cut the flesh lengthwise into fourths. Cut away the central hard core. Cut the flesh into chunks and add to the orange and passion fruit mixture. Cover and, if you are not serving at once, let the fruit chill.

Cut the pomegranate into fourths and, using your fingers or a teaspoon, remove the red seeds from the membrane. Cover and let chill until ready to serve—do not add too early to the fruit cocktail because the seeds discolor the other fruit.

Just before serving, peel and slice the banana, add to the fruit cocktail with the pomegranate seeds, and mix thoroughly. Serve at once.

melon & strawberry salad

serves 4

ingredients
½ iceberg lettuce, shredded
1 small honeydew melon
2 cups strawberries, sliced
2-inch/5-cm piece cucumber,
    thinly sliced
fresh mint sprigs, to garnish

for the dressing
scant 1 cup plain yogurt
2 inch/5 cm piece cucumber, peeled
a few fresh mint leaves
½ tsp finely grated lime or lemon rind
pinch of superfine sugar
3–4 ice cubes

Arrange the shredded lettuce on 4 serving plates.

Cut the melon lengthwise into fourths. Scoop out the seeds and cut through the flesh down to the skin at 1-inch/2.5-cm intervals. Cut the melon close to the skin and detach the flesh.

Place the chunks of melon on the beds of lettuce with the strawberry and cucumber slices.

To make the dressing, put the yogurt, cucumber, mint leaves, lime or lemon rind, superfine sugar, and ice cubes into a blender or food processor. Blend together for about 15 seconds until smooth. Alternatively, chop the cucumber and mint finely, crush the ice cubes, and combine with the other ingredients.

Serve the salad with a little dressing poured over it. Garnish with sprigs of fresh mint.

almonds: beansprout, apricot & almond salad 182
anchovies
　anchovy & olive salad 146
　broiled bell pepper salad 37
　Caesar salad 14
　Russian salad 138
　salad Niçoise 118
apples
　green fruit salad 209
　nutty beet salad 33
　salmon & avocado salad 129
　spring clean salad 174
　Waldorf summer chicken salad 66
apricots: bean sprout, apricot, & almond salad 182
artichokes
　artichoke & prosciutto salad 82
　melon, chorizo & artichoke salad 90
arugula 10
　asparagus & tomato salad 185
　avocado salad 186
　chicken, cheese, & arugula salad 106
　mussel salad 157
　roast pork & pumpkin salad 113
　salad with garlic dressing 54
　smoked chicken & cranberry salad 89
　smoked salmon & wild arugula salad 149
　tomato salad with feta cheese 38
　tuna & avocado salad 133
　warm pasta salad 57
asparagus
　asparagus & tomato salad 185
　prosciutto with melon & asparagus 70
avocados
avocado salad 186
　salmon & avocado salad 129
　smoked chicken & cranberry salad 89
　smoked chicken salad with avocado & tarragon
　　dressing 110
　smoked salmon & wild arugula salad 149
　tomato, mozzarella & avocado salad 197
　tuna & avocado salad 133

bacon & ham
　artichoke & prosciutto salad 82
　chef's salad 69
　crispy spinach & bacon 101
　prosciutto with melon & asparagus 70
　walnut, pear & crispy bacon salad 78
　warm mushroom, spinach, & pancetta salad 98
bananas: exotic fruit cocktail 218
beans & pulses
　chickpea & tomato salad 177
　lima bean, onion & herb salad, with spicy
　　sausage 85
　sweet potato & bean salad 49
　three bean salad 201
　tuna & two-bean salad 122
　see also fava beans; green beans; kidney beans;
　　lentils
bean sprouts
　bean sprout, apricot, & almond salad 182
　roast duck salad 97
　smoked chicken salad with avocado & tarragon
　　dressing 110
　Thai-style chicken salad 102
beef
　rare roast beef pasta salad 94
　roast beef salad 77
　warm beef Niçoise 73
beet
　Cajun chicken salad 74
　nutty beet salad 33
　red bell pepper & radicchio salad 173
　red & green salad 21
　three bean salad 201
beet greens 10
Belgian endive: spring clean salad 174
bell peppers
　broiled bell pepper & goat cheese salad 41
　broiled bell pepper salad 37

Italian salad 58
layered chicken salad 93
mussel salad 157
red bell pepper & radicchio salad 173
roast chicken with pesto cream salad 114
roast duck salad 97
roasted garlic, sweet potato, broiled eggplant, &
　bell pepper salad with mozzarella 22
roasted vegetable salad 198
salad with garlic dressing 54
succatash salad 202
sweet & sour fish salad 158
tuna & avocado salad 133
tuna & herbed fusilli salad 150
warm beef Niçoise 73
wild rice salad with cucumber & orange 170
zucchini & mint salad 194
broiled bell pepper & goat cheese salad 41
broiled bell pepper salad 37
broiled lamb with yogurt & herb dressing 109
buckwheat noodle salad with smoked tofu 193

cabbage
　buckwheat noodle salad with smoked tofu 193
　papaya salad 217
Caesar salad 14
Cajun chicken salad 74
cantaloupe & crab salad 142
capers
　broiled bell pepper & goat cheese salad 41
　celeriac rémoulade with crab 166
　mozzarella salad with sun-dried tomatoes 18
　Russian salad 138
　seared swordfish with fresh tomato salsa 162
Capri salad 62
carrots
　buckwheat noodle salad with smoked tofu 193
　orecchiette salad with pears & bleu cheese 53
　Russian salad 138
　sweet potato & bean salad 49
celeriac rémoulade with crab 166
celery
　chicken, cheese, & arugula salad 106
　duck & radish salad 105
　roast chicken with pesto cream salad 114
　salad with garlic dressing 54
　shrimp cocktail salad 165
　spring clean salad 174
　sweet potato & bean salad 49
　Waldorf summer chicken salad 66
　zucchini & mint salad 194
cheese
　avocado salad 186
　Caesar salad 14
　chef's salad 69
　chicken, cheese & arugula salad 106
　green bean & walnut salad 29
　orecchiette salad with pears & bleu cheese 53
　pear & Roquefort salad 206
　prosciutto with melon & asparagus 70
　spinach salad with bleu cheese dressing 205
　see also feta cheese; goat cheese; mozzarella
chef's salad 69
chicken
　Cajun chicken salad 74
　chef's salad 69
　chicken, cheese & arugula salad 106
　layered chicken salad 93
　roast chicken with pesto cream salad 114
　smoked chicken & cranberry salad 89
　smoked chicken salad with avocado & tarragon
　　dressing 110
　Thai-style chicken salad 102
　Waldorf summer chicken salad 66
　warm chicken liver salad 81
chickpea & tomato salad 177
chiles
　buckwheat noodle salad with smoked tofu 193
　chickpea & tomato salad 177
　chiled shrimp with pineapple & papaya salsa 161

lima bean, onion, & herb salad, with spicy
　sausage 85
Mexican tomato salad 45
papaya salad 217
roast duck salad 97
seafood & spinach salad 153
sweet & sour fish salad 158
Thai noodle salad 46
Thai-style chicken salad 102
tuna & avocado salad 133
chives
　broiled lamb with yogurt & herb dressing 109
　layered chicken salad 93
　mussel salad 157
　Neapolitan seafood salad 154
　pear & Roquefort salad 206
　potato salad 61
　spinach salad with bleu cheese dressing 205
　turkey & rice salad 86
chorizo
　lima bean, onion, & herb salad, with spicy
　　sausage 85
　melon, chorizo & artichoke salad 90
cockles: Neapolitan seafood salad 154
coconut
　coconut shrimp with cucumber salad 130
　roast duck salad 97
couscous: raspberry & feta salad with couscous 50
crab
　cantaloupe & crab salad 142
　celeriac rémoulade with crab 166
cranberries
　smoked chicken & cranberry salad 89
　three bean salad 201
crispy spinach & bacon 101
cucumber
　chicken, cheese, & arugula salad 106
　coconut shrimp with cucumber salad 130
　melon & strawberry salad 221
　rare roast beef salad pasta 94
　roast duck salad 97
　salad with garlic dressing 54
　tabbouleh 190
　traditional Greek salad 17
　warm pasta salad 57
　wild rice salad with cucumber & orange 170

duck
　duck & radish salad 105
　roast duck salad 97

eggplants
　roasted garlic, sweet potato, broiled eggplant, &
　　bell pepper salad with mozzarella 22
　roasted vegetable salad 198
eggs
　broiled bell pepper salad 37
　Caesar salad 14
　chef's salad 69
　fava bean salad 42
　Russian salad 138
　salad Niçoise 118
　warm beef Niçoise 73
exotic fruit cocktail 218

fava beans
　fava bean salad 42
　Russian salad 138
fennel & orange salad 178
feta cheese
　fava bean salad 42
　raspberry & feta salad with couscous 50
　roast pork & pumpkin salad 113
　three bean salad 201
　tomato salad with feta cheese 38
　traditional Greek salad 17
fig & watermelon salad 213
fish
　sweet & sour fish salad 158
　see also individual fish & seafood

fruit salad
  exotic fruit cocktail 218
  green fruit salad 209
  tropical fruit salad 210

garlic
  roasted garlic, sweet potato, grilled eggplant, &
    bell pepper salad with mozzarella 22
  salad with garlic dressing 54
goat cheese
  broiled bell pepper & goat cheese salad 41
  warm red lentil salad with goat cheese 26
grapes
  bean sprout, apricot, & almond salad 182
  chicken, cheese, & arugula salad 106
  fig & watermelon salad 213
  green fruit salad 209
  melon & mango salad 214
green beans
  green bean & walnut salad 29
  roast beef salad 77
  roast pork & pumpkin salad 113
  salad Niçoise 118
  tuna & fresh vegetable salad 125
  tuna & two-bean salad 122
  warm beef Niçoise 73
  zucchini & mint salad 194
green fruit salad 209

herbs
  broiled lamb with yogurt & herb dressing 109
  herby potato salad 189
  lima bean, onion, & herb salad with spicy
    sausage 85
  red onion, tomato, & herb salad 30
  smoked chicken salad with avocado & tarragon
    dressing 110
  tuna & herbed fusilli salad 150
  zucchini & mint salad 194
herby potato salad 189
honey
  artichoke & prosciutto salad 82
  broiled lamb with yogurt & herb dressing 109
  fig & watermelon salad 213
  green fruit salad 209
  melon & mango salad 214
  mussel salad 157
  rare roast beef pasta salad 94
  shrimp & rice salad 145
  sweet & sour fish salad 158
  tuna & herbed fusilli salad 150
  walnut, pear, & crispy bacon salad 78

Italian salad 58

kidney beans
  Mexican tomato salad 45
  three bean salad 201
kiwi fruit: green fruit salad 209

lamb: broiled lamb with yogurt & herb dressing 109
layered chicken salad 93
lentils
  lentil & tuna salad 121
  warm new potato & lentil salad 181
  warm red lentil salad with goat cheese 26
lima bean, onion, & herb salad, with spicy
  sausage 85
limes
  cantaloupe & crab salad 142
  duck & radish salad 105
  fig & watermelon salad 213
  Mexican tomato salad 45
  papaya salad 217
  rare roast beef pasta salad 94
  roast duck salad 97
  shrimp & rice salad 145
  smoked salmon & wild arugula salad 149
  Thai noodle salad 46
  Thai-style chicken salad 102
  tuna & herbed fusilli salad 150

lobster salad 137

mâche 10
mangoes
  Cajun chicken salad 74
  melon & mango salad 214
  shrimp & mango salad 126
  shrimp & rice salad 145
  tropical fruit salad 210
melon
  avocado salad 186
  cantaloupe & crab salad 142
  fig & watermelon salad 213
  green fruit salad 209
  melon, chorizo & artichoke salad 90
  melon & mango salad 214
  melon & strawberry salad 221
  prosciutto with melon & asparagus 70
  spring clean salad 174
mesclun 11
Mexican tomato salad 45
mixed mushroom salad 25
mizuna 11
  asparagus & tomato salad 185
mozzarella
  Capri salad 62
  Italian salad 58
  mozzarella salad with sun-dried tomatoes 18
  roasted garlic, sweet potato, broiled eggplant, &
    bell pepper salad with mozzarella 22
  three-color salad 34
  tomato, mozzarella, & avocado salad 197
mushrooms
  mixed mushroom salad 25
  Russian salad 138
  Thai noodle salad 46
  tuna & fresh vegetable salad 125
  turkey & rice salad 86
  warm mushroom, spinach, & pancetta salad 98
mussels
  mussel salad 157
  Neapolitan seafood salad 154
  seafood salad 141
  seafood & spinach salad 153
mustard
  artichoke & prosciutto salad 82
  asparagus & tomato salad 185
  Cajun chicken salad 74
  celeriac rémoulade with crab 166
  chicken, cheese, & arugula salad 106
  lentil & tuna salad 121
  lobster salad 137
  melon, chorizo & artichoke salad 90
  mussel salad 157
  roast beef salad 77
  roast pork & pumpkin salad 113
  succatash salad 202
  three bean salad 201
  tomato, mozzarella & avocado salad 197
  tomato, salmon & shrimp salad 134
  tuna & herbed fusilli salad 150
  warm beef Niçoise 73
  warm chicken liver salad 81
  warm mushroom, spinach, & pancetta salad 98
  warm pasta salad 57

nasturtium 11
Neapolitan seafood salad 154
noodles
  buckwheat noodle salad with smoked tofu 193
  Thai noodle salad 46
nuts
  bean sprout, apricot, & almond salad 182
  nutty beet salad 33
  papaya salad 217
  roast beef salad 77
  shrimp & rice salad 145
  three bean salad 201
  turkey & rice salad 86
  see also pine kernels; walnuts

nutty beet salad 33

olives
  anchovy & olive salad 146
  artichoke & prosciutto salad 82
  asparagus & tomato salad 185
  broiled bell pepper salad 37
  Capri salad 62
  herby potato salad 189
  Italian salad 58
  roast beef salad 77
  salad Niçoise 118
  seared swordfish with fresh tomato salsa 162
  tomato, mozzarella, & avocado salad 197
  tomato salad with feta cheese 38
  traditional Greek salad 17
  warm beef Niçoise 73
onion
  lima bean, onion, & herb salad with spicy
    sausage 85
  red onion, tomato, & herb salad 30
oranges
  exotic fruit cocktail 218
  fennel & orange salad 178
  fig & watermelon salad 213
  green fruit salad 209
  red & green salad 21
  spinach salad with bleu cheese dressing 205
  tropical fruit salad 210
  wild rice salad with cucumber & orange 170
orecchiette salad with pears & bleu cheese 53

papayas
  chiled shrimp with pineapple & papaya salsa 161
  papaya salad 217
  tropical fruit salad 210
passion fruit
  exotic fruit cocktail 218
  melon & mango salad 214
pasta
  Italian salad 58
  Neapolitan seafood salad 154
  orecchiette salad with pears & bleu cheese 53
  rare roast beef pasta salad 94
  roast beef salad 77
  tuna & herbed fusilli salad 150
  warm pasta salad 57
pears
  orecchiette salad with pears & bleu cheese 53
  pear & Roquefort salad 206
  walnut, pear & crispy bacon salad 78
pesto: roast chicken with pesto cream salad 114
pine nuts
  asparagus & tomato salad 185
  Italian salad 58
  mixed mushroom salad 25
  raspberry & feta salad with couscous 50
  roast pork & pumpkin salad 113
pineapple
  chiled shrimp with pineapple & papaya salsa 161
  exotic fruit cocktail 218
  sweet & sour fish salad 158
  tropical fruit salad 210
pomegranates: exotic fruit cocktail 218
pork
  roast pork & pumpkin salad 113
  Thai noodle salad 46
potatoes
  herby potato salad 189
  layered chicken salad 93
  potato salad 61
  Russian salad 138
  salmon & avocado salad 129
  Thai-style chicken salad 102
  tuna & avocado salad 133
  warm beef Niçoise 73
  warm new potato & lentil salad 181
prosciutto
  artichoke & prosciutto salad 82
  prosciutto with melon & asparagus 70
pumpkin: roast pork & pumpkin salad 113

quinoa: tabbouleh 190
radicchio 11
  avocado salad 186
  cantaloupe & crab salad 142
  lobster salad 137
  mussel salad 157
  orecchiette salad with pears & bleu cheese 53
  pear & Roquefort salad 206
  red bell pepper & radicchio salad 173
  roast beef salad 77
radishes
  Cajun chicken salad 74
  duck & radish salad 105
  red bell pepper & radicchio salad 173
  salad with garlic dressing 54
  three bean salad 201
rare roast beef pasta salad 94
raspberries
  prosciutto with melon & asparagus 70
  raspberry & feta salad with couscous 50
red & green salad 21
red bell pepper & radicchio salad 173
red chard 11
red onion, tomato, & herb salad 30
rice
  coconut shrimp with cucumber salad 130
  shrimp & rice salad 145
  turkey & rice salad 86
  wild rice salad with cucumber & orange 170
roast beef salad 77
roast chicken with pesto cream salad 114
roast duck salad 97
roast pork & pumpkin salad 113
roasted garlic, sweet potato, broiled eggplant, &
  bell pepper salad with mozzarella 22
roasted vegetable salad 198
romaine lettuce 11
  Caesar salad 14
  chickpea & tomato salad 177
Russian salad 138

salad greens 10-11
  anchovy & olive salad 146
  asparagus & tomato salad 185
  Caesar salad 14
  Cajun chicken salad 74
  chef's salad 69
  duck & radish salad 105
  lima bean, onion, & herb salad with spicy
    sausage 85
  melon & mango salad 214
  melon & strawberry salad 221
  mixed mushroom salad 25
  mozzarella salad with sun-dried tomatoes 18
  Neapolitan seafood salad 154
  nutty beet salad 33
  orecchiette salad with pears & bleu cheese 53
  papaya salad 217
  pear & Roquefort salad 206
  prosciutto with melon & asparagus 70
  roast chicken with pesto cream salad 114
  roast duck salad 97
  roasted garlic, sweet potato, broiled eggplant, &
    bell pepper salad with mozzarella 22
  salad Niçoise 118
  salmon & avocado salad 129
  shrimp cocktail salad 165
  shrimp & mango salad 126
  smoked chicken & cranberry salad 89
  sweet potato & bean salad 49
  three bean salad 201
  tomato, salmon, & shrimp salad 134
  traditional Greek salad 17
  tuna & two-bean salad 122
  Waldorf summer chicken salad 66
  warm beef Niçoise 73
  warm chicken liver salad 81
  see also arugula; chicory; mizuna; radicchio;
    romaine lettuce; spinach; watercress
salad leaf preparation 11

salad leaf storage 11
salad Niçoise 118
salad with garlic dressing 54
salmon
  salmon & avocado salad 129
  smoked salmon & wild arugula salad 149
  tomato, salmon, & shrimp salad 134
sausage: see chorizo
scallops
  seafood & spinach salad 153
  seafood salad 141
seafood & spinach salad 153
seafood salad 141, 154
seared swordfish with fresh tomato salsa 162
sesame seeds
  broiled lamb with yogurt & herb dressing 109
  buckwheat noodle salad with smoked tofu 193
  Cajun chicken salad 74
  duck & radish salad 105
  tuna & avocado salad 133
shrimp
  chiled shrimp with pineapple & papaya salsa 161
  coconut shrimp with cucumber salad 130
  Russian salad 138
  seafood & spinach salad 153
  shrimp cocktail salad 165
  shrimp & mango salad 126
  shrimp & rice salad 145
  Thai noodle salad 46
  tomato, salmon, & shrimp salad 134
smoked chicken & cranberry salad 89
smoked chicken salad with avocado & tarragon
  dressing 110
smoked salmon & wild arugula salad 149
snow peas: turkey & rice salad 86
spinach
  crispy spinach & bacon 101
  red & green salad 21
  salmon & avocado salad 129
  seafood & spinach salad 153
  spinach salad with bleu cheese dressing 205
  warm mushroom, spinach, & pancetta salad 98
  warm red lentil salad with goat cheese 26
spring clean salad 174
squid
  Neapolitan seafood salad 154
  seafood salad 141
strawberries
  melon & strawberry salad 221
  tropical fruit salad 210
string beans: succatash salad 202
succatash salad 202
sugar snap peas: smoked chicken & cranberry
  salad 89
sunflower seeds: spinach salad with bleu cheese
  dressing 205
sweet & sour fish salad 158
sweet potatoes
  roasted garlic, sweet potato, broiled eggplant, &
    bell pepper salad with mozzarella 22
  sweet potato & bean salad 49
sweetcorn
  Russian salad 138
  succatash salad 202
  Thai-style chicken salad 102
swordfish: seared swordfish with fresh tomato
  salsa 162

tabbouleh 190
Thai noodle salad 46
Thai-style chicken salad 102
three bean salad 201
three-color salad 34
tofu: buckwheat noodle salad with smoked tofu 193
tomatoes
  anchovy & olive salad 146
  artichoke & prosciutto salad 82
  asparagus & tomato salad 185
  Capri salad 62
  chef's salad 69
  chickpea & tomato salad 177

herby potato salad 189
Italian salad 58
layered chicken salad 93
lentil & tuna salad 121
lima bean, onion, & herb salad with spicy
  sausage 85
Mexican tomato salad 45
mozzarella salad with sun-dried tomatoes 18
Neapolitan seafood salad 154
orecchiette salad with pears & bleu cheese 53
papaya salad 217
rare roast beef pasta salad 94
red onion, tomato, & herb salad 30
salad with garlic dressing 54
salad Niçoise 118
salmon & avocado salad 129
seared swordfish with fresh tomato salsa 162
smoked chicken salad with avocado & tarragon
  dressing 110
sweet potato & bean salad 49
tabbouleh 190
three bean salad 201
three-color salad 34
tomato, mozzarella, & avocado salad 197
tomato salad with feta cheese 38
tomato, salmon, & shrimp salad 134
traditional Greek salad 17
tuna & avocado salad 133
tuna & fresh vegetable salad 125
tuna & herbed fusilli salad 150
tuna & two-bean salad 122
warm beef Niçoise 73
warm pasta salad 57
wild rice salad with cucumber & orange 170
tongue: chef's salad 69
traditional Greek salad 17
tropical fruit salad 210
trout: sweet & sour fish salad 158
tuna
  lentil & tuna salad 121
  salad Niçoise 118
  tuna & avocado salad 133
  tuna & fresh vegetable salad 125
  tuna & herbed fusilli salad 150
  tuna & two-bean salad 122
turkey & rice salad 86
turnips: Russian salad 138

Waldorf summer chicken salad 66
walnuts
  Cajun chicken salad 74
  chicken, cheese & arugula salad 106
  green bean & walnut salad 29
  orecchiette salad with pears & bleu cheese 53
  salmon & avocado salad 129
  Waldorf summer chicken salad 66
  walnut, pear & crispy bacon salad 78
warm beef Niçoise 73
warm chicken liver salad 81
warm mushroom, spinach, & pancetta salad 98
warm new potato & lentil salad 181
warm pasta salad 57
warm red lentil salad with goat cheese 26
watercress
  melon & mango salad 214
  smoked chicken & cranberry salad 89
  smoked chicken salad with avocado & tarragon
    dressing 110
  sweet & sour fish salad 158
  walnut, pear & crispy bacon salad 78
  zucchini & mint salad 194
wild rice salad with cucumber & orange 170

yogurt: grilled lamb with yogurt & herb dressing 109

zucchini
  layered chicken salad 93
  raspberry & feta salad with couscous 50
  roasted vegetable salad 198
  tuna & fresh vegetable salad 125
zucchini & mint salad 194